ADRIAN
BENJA

TRUE CRIME GERMANY 2

REAL SHOCKING AND UNKNOWN
CRIMINAL CASES FROM EUROPE

Imprint

uthors: Adrian Langenscheid, Benjamin Rickert, Harmke Horst

ISBN:
"978-3-98661-055-5" True Crime Germany 2 English Paperback

Editing: Hannah Thier, B.A. MSc.
Translation: Lea Prescher

1st edition June 2022

Cover image: © Canva (canva.com)
Cover design: Pixa Heros, Stuttgart

Some dialogues and statements of the persons appearing in this book are not quoted verbatim, but reproduced according to the sense and content.

ADRIAN LANGENSCHEID
BENJAMIN RICKERT

TRUE CRIME GERMANY 2

REAL SHOCKING AND UNKNOWN CRIMINAL CASES FROM EUROPE

About this book:

Stone-cold serial killers, doomed family dramas, tragic kidnappings, vile torture, and unscrupulous abuse: ten shocking True Crime short stories on true crime cases from Germany.

Captivated, stunned, amazed, and moved to tears, you will question everything you thought you knew about human nature. Life writes horrifying stories, and this book brings them together. Immerse yourself in the shocking world of true crime and real crime!

About the authors:

Adrian Langenscheid is the author of the successful True Crime International book series. His books have achieved bestseller status beyond the borders of Germany. Together with thriller author Benjamin Rickert, the two true crime experts follow up the remarkable successes of their predecessors with the seventh volume of the series.

Inhalt

I have almost forgotten the taste of fears;
The time has been, my senses would have cool'd
To hear a night-shriek; and my fell of hair
Would at a dismal treatise rouse and stir
As life were in't; have supp'd full with horrors;
Direness, familiar to my slaughterous thoughts
Cannot once start me.

- William Shakespeare (1564-1616), English playwright, lyricist, and actor

Preface

I would have believed him to be capable of a great deal, but this? Never. I trusted him and I could talk to him about everything. But then it turned out that he was really a criminal. I could not think clearly. All these years I thought I knew how he thought and acted. This news hit me with the force of an armored fist.

The policewoman behind the desk looks deeply into my eyes through her square glasses. My friend is accused of sexually assaulting minors over an extended period of time. Through my testimony, they seek to get a picture of his personality.

As their words reach my ear, I don't know where to put my feelings. I am shocked, disappointed, and equally confused, because I would trust the person with anything - but something like this? Never! I truthfully state this to the policewoman.

Only he and the victim know whether my friend really committed the acts of which he was accused. Although he was convicted, he maintains his innocence to this day.

With my face buried in my hands, I sit at the tram stop following the pronouncement of the verdict and ask myself: Isn't it always the case that behind the bourgeois facade of acquaintances, the cordial behavior of dear friends, or the helpfulness of friendly neighbors, unspeakably deep abysses often open up?

Benjamin Rickert

If one can›t be a great artist or a great soldier, the next best thing is to be a great criminal.

- F. Scott Fitzgerald (1896-1940),
American Author

CHAPTER 1

Crime weapon telephone

The tall, lanky man, dressed in fine threads, paces restlessly up and down his small apartment room. Nervously, he runs his right hand over his mouth. "What am I going to do?" he mutters to himself. His eyes wander back to the two-light window that overlooks the street. A police car had parked in front of his apartment building a few moments ago. The man is sure that the law enforcement officers want to get to him. And then what? His greatest fear is going to jail. A panicky, paralyzing feeling comes over him at this thought. Mortal fear. It is impossible for him to turn himself in. Suddenly, the man opens his eyes and twists his lips into a smile. He has an idea. He quickly grabs a piece of paper and a pen and scribbles a few raspy words. Next, he tears off a strip of scotch tape and rushes to his apartment door with the note in his hand. He opens the door a crack, hastily sticks the note under the peephole, quietly closes the door, and then takes a few steps back. What happens now is out of his hands. It could work, but it could also mean the end of his freedom. He holds his breath and listens intently into the hallway. Someone must have opened the front door for the police officers because he hears feet in heavy shoes coming up the stairs. Just outside his apartment door, the footsteps fall silent. The man holds his breath. He hears the two officers murmuring as they seem to read his note. Cautiously, he creeps to the door peephole and peers out… right into the eye of a police officer. He recoils - reflexively presses a hand over his mouth; only with difficulty can he suppress an outcry. "No Klaus, it says here that Postel is away for two weeks. Let's pass it on to the control center. What do you want to do?" a male voice asks. Then again heavy footsteps trudging down the stairs. The man raises his eyebrows in disbelief. That he is intellectually superior to most people, he has long known, but the stupidity of others really does seem boundless. The morons didn't even bother to knock. They just believed his scribbled note. The genius hurriedly grabs a suitcase from his closet and throws in some clothes and the most necessary things for an escape. A glance through the door peephole confirms the coast is clear. After pulling the apartment door into the lock behind him, he turns back to his note: "Dear Peter, I'm with Susanne. Will be back in two weeks. Gert." He shakes his head and smiles triumphantly before leaving the apartment building at a busy pace with his packed belongings. He is no longer safe in Berlin, so the dapperly dressed, charming-looking man goes on the run.

Gert Postel, the only child of a mechanic and a seamstress, was born in Bremen on June 18, 1958. Growing up in the tranquil village of Stuhr, his relationship with his father is strained and loveless. On the other hand, his relationship with his mother is intimate. She is adored by her son who admires her for striving for something higher, something she will never be able to achieve with her husband's small salary as a simple laborer. Postel finishes secondary school and then attends night school. He's unable to do anything with mathematics and numbers but nevertheless, Gert makes it - he catches up on his secondary school leaving certificate. His career aspirations: policeman or customs officer. Unfortunately, his father is against this. He wants his son to work for the German Federal Post Office. Gert obeys his father and by the end of the 1070s, completes his training as a letter carrier He performs impeccably, but is not happy as a letter carrier. Postel, like his mother, also feels called to become something higher…something he can never achieve with his current school education. It is as if the striving and failure of his beloved mother is being repeated in Gert's own life.

In 1979, father and son discover their mother dead, hanging by a rope, dangling over the bathtub. A shock, an unspeakable loss that young Gert will never overcome for the rest of his life. It is also the birth of his hatred for psychiatrists and doctors in general. Gert believes he knows why his mother, who suffered from depression, chose suicide: a doctor had prescribed her drugs to increase her drive, but not to relieve depression, thus giving her the physical strength to take her own life in the first place. Truly an unforgivable misjudgment of Ms. Postel's state of mind and the turning point in the letter carrier's life.

Gert wants to belong to a better, more prestigious milieu, so the unhappy delivery man starts reading renowned daily newspapers and making contacts with academics, doctors, and lawyers. Postel chooses a sauna as his place of action. He knows it is frequented mainly by people who belong to the milieu to which he also wants to belong. All people are equal when they go to the sauna. It is a place where people can talk freely, make themselves look bigger than they really are, and make new friends. His plan works.

Moving forward, Gert Postel tries to gain professional positions using both smaller and larger shenanigans. The contacts he makes in the sauna serve as door openers because in the absence of a qualifying education, he has no business or experience with the jobs he accepts. If he is found out, however, only small fines await him because of his unauthorized use of an academic degree or the like. Nothing can stop Gert Postel from proving time and again that he is vastly superior to other people, especially those people who believe they are better just because they received an academic education. After all, he believes, it is clear to everyone that studying medicine is not an educationally beneficial course of study. Gert Postel sees it this way: Of course, doctors can also be educated, even though they are physicians. But this is an absolute exception, especially in the discipline of psychiatry.

It is the end of 1982 when Postel, now 24 years old, applies for the advertised position of deputy medical officer in Flensburg. As part of the process, Postel calmly submits falsified documents: The former letter carrier now calls himself Dr. med. Clemens Bartholdy, the son of a medical councilor and a medical director who is in his thirties. Bartholdy has an unbroken curriculum vitae, which Postel supports with examination results and certificates. He does this in a criminal way quite cleverly: Postel really does present a genuine doctoral certificate. To do this, the young man calls the medical school in Hanover and pretends to be an employee of a court in Bremen. He said he was calling because the court in question was currently conducting proceedings against a defendant on charges of forgery and fraud. In the context of the proceedings, a stamped and sealed doctoral certificate is required. To ensure that no mischief can be committed with it, the court will send a messenger to pick up this document.

Postel then gets into his car and sets off for Hanover to receive the letter, disguised as a courier.

During the job interview at the health department in Flensburg, Postel, alias Bartholdy, answers the question about which topic he had earned his doctorate in psychology in with "The cognitive distortion in stereotypical judgment formation." In truth, a string of empty phrases, but Postel knows that someone with two doctorates will not be questioned.

The lie construct pays off and Postel gets the job. Wolfgang Wodrag, the head of the office, overlooks the fact that he does not yet have all the necessary documents from the doctor. Postel soon realizes why Wodrag was only too willing to give him the post of deputy medical officer in Flensburg: From now on, Dr. Bartholdy is responsible for conducting the health examinations of prostitutes and strippers, among other things. This is a task that most doctors like to shirk. Bartholdy does not necessarily like this field of activity either, but in his new office, he is able to make a difference. While he is on duty, only 10% of applications for psychiatric placements are approved instead of over 95%. Though he often appears insecure to his colleagues in the health department, he does not make any serious mistakes because the wrong doctor compensates for his professional ignorance by diligently investigating. He calls family doctors and asks for the findings of his patient in question. In this way, he compiles his “own” medical reports. The head of the office, Wodrag, does not suspect anything because if there is one thing that the fake medical officer Bartholdy is good at, it is rambling. Postel becomes more confident and self-assured every day, so he applies for a job at the university neurological clinic in Kiel. Indeed, he is chosen for the advertised post from a large number of applicants. Yet even if one, and least probably he himself, may hardly believe it, even Gert Postel is not infallible. One day the aspiring “doctor” loses his wallet in front of the entrance to the police station in Flensburg, of all places. Postel had frequently worked with the officers there as a medical officer. The police officers were astonished when they opened the wallet they found, for inside it contained an identity card in the name of Gert Postel and a service card in the name of Dr. Clemens Bartholdy, each with identical passport photos. The ball starts rolling and a court case follows but the punishment for the false public health officer is relatively mild - another fine. Thi is also most likely because they tried to prevent the trial from being blown out of proportion and damaging the reputation of the Flensburger even more.

Towards the end of the 1980s, Postel makes a new plan: he wants to study Catholic theology in Münster and become a priest. The documents and certificates required for enrolment are, of course, all forged. Clear rules and a fixed hierarchy are what the cunning young man appreciates about the church, even if one might not necessarily imagine such a sly fellow with his twisted values as God's spokesperson. Sure, he could have joined the German army, but digging in the dirt and cleaning guns are not tasks for Gert Postel. During his studies, he proves that he puts his worldly existence above that of everyone else. He argues that he is entitled to a private audience with Pope John Paul II in Rome and indeed, the aspiring priest manages to persuade the Bishop of Münster to issue him a letter of recommendation. Postel travels to Rome and meets the venerable Pope. A souvenir photo is taken before the theology student flies back to Münster. There, however, a nasty surprise awaits him: while he was in Rome, the rector of the student college got wind of the fraudulent machinations and the falsified application documents of the trained letter carrier. He is expelled from the Catholic college. The would-be priest did not suffer any legal consequences.

In 1993, Postel moves to the cosmopolitan city of Berlin. He hadn't even settled in before he was caught by a store detective stealthily making a newspaper disappear into his jacket in a supermarket. The Berlin public prosecutor's office relentlessly charges the shoplifter with theft, but the cunning thief knows how to wriggle out of his predicament. He resorts to his favorite weapon: the telephone. It is a characteristic of his modus operandi that he always first seeks telephone contact with people whose good nature and trustworthiness he then shamelessly exploits. Postel sits up straight, clears his throat briefly, and adjusts his glasses before quickly pressing a few keys on the phone. He listens intently to the ringing until someone at the other end of the line finally picks up the receiver. "Judge Blöddorn, presiding judge of the court of lay assessors in Hamburg," Gert Postel confidently introduces himself to the lead prosecutor in his trial for the theft. "I'm calling you about the proceedings against Gert Postel. Here in Hamburg, there has been a main hearing against the delinquent. He was sentenced to two years in prison." He claims this because he knows very well that the proceedings will then be discontinued in Berlin, since the expected punishment is disproportionate to the prison term imposed. The public prosecutor thanks Judge Blöddorn for the call. She will now suggest that the pending proceedings in Berlin against Postel be discontinued. But Judge Blöddorn plays it safe, he calls other court employees in Berlin and presents his fairy tale of a trial that has taken place and the prison sentence that has been imposed. As happens so often he achieves exactly what he wants. No one confirms whether the file number mentioned is correct or whether a Judge Blöddorn from Hamburg even exists. The case against Postel is dropped.

It is 1995 when Gert Postel decides to return to a regular job. He applies for an advertised position as a senior physician in a psychiatric clinic in Leipzig.

Beforehand, he makes a phone call as Prof. Dr. von Berg, senior consultant at the university neurological clinic in Münster. Dr. von Berg calls Leipzig and tells the senior director of the psychiatric institution that he has discovered the job advertisement and would now, collegially, like to recommend a doctor from his clinic for the post. He would prefer to continue employing him himself in his institute, but the clinic staff would have to be drastically reduced for cost reasons. Dr. Gert Postel is soon on his way to Saxony, the former GDR, to personally introduce himself to the director.

The talented actor returns once again as a fake doctor; the role he most loves to play. More self-confident than ever, he no longer uses a pseudonym. So sure is he of his cause by now and somehow, he is not entirely wrong because Postel gets the job without having to make any special effort. His falsified credentials speak for themselves. His charming and engaging manner takes care of the rest. The director, as well as the other doctors, are immediately taken with the new colleague from West-Germany, who is responsible for the clinic's neurological and psychiatric departments.

But soon, there is friction between Postel and the other employees. They whisper amongst themselves that Dr. Postel thinks he knows everything and knows it better, a "know it-all". He also appears lazy because he always lets his subordinates do all the medical examinations, medication displays, and other things that have to be done in a clinic's daily routine. He himself just hands everything off, devotes himself mainly to administrative tasks and writes reports on his patients. With this task, Gert Postel eventually takes it even further, acting as a psychiatric expert witness in numerous court cases. His task is to assess the culpability of the accused. Dr. Postel appears so self-confident that no one ever doubts him or even dares to question his authority. It is a wonder that during his time as a fake doctor, Gert Postel cannot be proven to have had a case in which a patient suffered health damage because of him. Eventually, he begins to ask himself whether he is perhaps an impostor among impostors. After all, his medical colleagues pretend that they are capable of curing people but if he, a letter carrier, is also capable of doing so, then perhaps the patients will simply get well, even though these psychiatric doctors exist? Postel sees this assumption as legitimation to continue his hustle and bustle without any hesitation.

In the summer of 1996, Dr. Postel is at a professional peak. He is satisfied with his work and about to be promoted to head of a forensic clinic in Dresden. Dr. Postel feels flattered but is nevertheless irritated by the offer and feigns modesty. He is still quite young and does not yet have the professional experience to hold such a post. In addition, he has only been working at the Leipzig clinic for six months. He relishes the fact that top-class physicians literally beg him, a letter carrier, to accept the position in Dresden because of his medical skills, but he declines the offer. Dr. Postel feels so comfortable in the clinic in Leipzig that the offer of a position as chief physician fails to appeal to him. But now it is only a matter of time before the impostor's lucky streak slowly begins to break.

The psychiatric clinic in Leipzig is planning to set up a day clinic so that it can also offer outpatient therapy. As chance would have it, during a visit home to Flensburg, a young assistant doctor tells her parents that Dr. Gert Postel is to head this new facility at the clinic. The young woman's father becomes suspicious - Postel? The name is all too familiar in Flensburg and has remained in the memory of many people because in 1982 and 1983 someone had posed as a doctor, Dr. med. Clemens Bartholdy. Wasn't the impostor also called Postel?

Then one morning, Dr. Gert Postel arrives at his workplace in the Leipzig clinic. He struts up to the chief physician's office as if it were the most natural thing in the world. He is the only one allowed to show up at his office unannounced at any time and is always welcome, but this morning everything is different. When Dr. Postel enters the anteroom, the secretary looks at him with a mixture of astonishment and incredulity. She draws the air sharply between her teeth and whispers excitedly, "For

God's sake, don't go in there. The boss is acting so strange today. I've never seen him like this before!" Postel looks at the stunned woman for a few seconds and then his face goes pale. A feeling of panic overcomes him and cold sweat begins to coat his body. He is busted. No words are needed, he just feels it and his intuition does not deceive him. He has worked in the clinic for a year and a half. He felt comfortable and was able to bask in the appreciation of his colleagues - but that is over now. He leaves the clinic in a hurry, gets into his car, and drives off. In his luggage: 80,000 DM that he had saved up. His destination: the big city of Berlin. He now must go into hiding. In the back of his mind is the fear of being locked up in a prison - a paralyzing fear, tantamount to panic.

But what had happened? The head physician of the clinic received a call from Flensburg and heard a sentence that brings the delinquent's tissue of lies crashing down: "You obviously don't know that your head doctor is a mailman."

Only a few steps away from Ku'damm, Postel rents a small apartment under a false name. Slowly, the driven impostor finds peace. For a while, the anonymity of the big city acts like a band-aid on a festering, aching wound. But eventually the wound tears open: It is the evening of November 24, 1997, when Postel's likeness flickers across the screen in the television program "Fahndungsakte." A few days later, the police arrive at Postel's door and read the attached note that the wanted fraudster is away for two weeks.

To savor his triumph over the "stupid" public servants, the first thing the fugitive does is go to a telephone booth. He calls the prosecutor responsible for this morning's disturbance. "Postel here. I wanted to complain. It wasn't very nice sending police officers to my house so early in the morning and disturbing me." "Oh, Mr. Postel! We finally caught you!" the prosecutor replies to him from the other side of the line. "And you're calling from police custody now?" the lawyer inquires. Postel laughs and tells him the story that took place just a few minutes earlier. The prosecutor, known as a calm man with a cool demeanor, loses his temper and begins to rant and rave, much to the delight of Gert Postel. He hangs up the phone, leaves the phone booth, and embarks on a flight that will take him across Germany over the next weeks and months. When he rents a place to stay, he likes using as pseudonyms the names of the prosecutors and detectives who, in the meantime, are feverishly searching for the swindler.

After eleven months, the fake doctor's escape ends in a telephone booth in Stuttgart. A judge friend of the fugitive lures him into a trap. She tells him that she is not well and expresses the wish that he should call her at certain times. Postel does her the favor until, during one of these phone calls, he suddenly looks down the barrel of a gun. Quickly and textbook-like, a task force surrounds the phone booth and rips open the door. Postel is perplexed. He never expected to be betrayed by this friend. After all, she already knew about his machinations before his fake application to the Leipzig psychiatric hospital and even visited him a few times at his workplace. The impostor drops the telephone receiver, which now dangles back and forth on its cord. There is an eerie silence before Postel slowly raises his hands above his head as a sign of his surrender. The game is over.

The trial of the fake doctor takes place in the Leipzig District Court with sixty-five cases of fraud and document forgery. It is a general reckoning and the result of a long career as an impostor. The media interest is great and the accused letter carrier basks in the flash of the photographers. He does not seem unhappy, for how could he be as the center of public interest? At the end of the trial, the verdict is passed in the name of the people: Postel is sentenced to a total term of four years of imprisonment.

Contrary to his fears, the convict does not find hisprison time to be torture. He uses his free time to study topics like Schopenhauer's philosophy. The reformed letter carrier has been free and on probation since 2001. He writes books and gives interviews and lectures about a time when he felt like an "impostor among impostors."

In the past we suffered from crime, now we suffer from laws.

- Publius Cornelius Tacitus (58 AD - 120 AD) -

CHAPTER 2

Torn from life

Anna T. makes her way to the Red City Hall in Berlin at just before 1 p.m. on January 29, 2018, to have lunch in the canteen. The 33-year-old works in the registry office in Berlin-Mitte, a few hundred meters away. The multi-lane Grunerstrasse runs between the two buildings, with a parking strip in the middle. Especially around noon, heavy traffic rushes across the street. Every second, one car after another shoots out of the tunnel near Alexanderplatz in the direction of Leipziger Strasse. Anyone who is careless here pays with their life.

Anna is aware of this, too, and proceeds accordingly as she crosses the road. When she reaches the median strip, she looks around. The road seems empty, except for a white Renault Clio that is about to squeeze into an empty parking space. From far away, T. hears a siren.

She puts her foot on the road and takes three steps as a police car comes barreling toward her from the right. The sound of the siren instantly reaches her eardrums at a deafening volume. In shock, T. jumps backwards and sees the police car crash into the driver's door of the white Renault Clio. Debris flies around and tires roll across the road. The police car pushes the Renault a few meters further, then both vehicles come to a halt. If Anna T. had hesitated even a second longer, she would probably now be lying under one of the cars.

After she has overcome her shock, the 33-year-old rushes to the driver's door of the completely demolished Renault Clio. Behind the steering wheel sits a young woman. Although she looks completely unharmed, she is not conscious. Anna T. tries to free the woman from the wreckage, but the door was so badly damaged in the collision that it cannot be opened. T. goes over to the passenger side; there, too, she fails. Another passerby rushes to the aid of the shocked eyewitness. While the latter tends to the injured woman and alerts the emergency doctor, T. unsuccessfully tries to stop passing cars to acquire a first-aid kit.

When the rescue workers arrive at the scene of the accident a few minutes later, it is already swarming with people. Someone had managed to free the young woman from the car and together they administer first aid. Grunerstrasse is cordoned off and colleagues of the traffic police record the facts of the case. The two men in the patrol car that approached T. were Chief Inspector Peter

G. and a young police trainee from the police headquarters not far from Alexanderplatz. Around three o'clock they were called to a robbery in the "Mall of Berlin", a shopping center at Leipziger Platz. The two police officers, who had just started their duty that day, switch on the blue light as well as the siren and drive at high speed through the tunnel that leads into Grunerstrasse. A few meters away, the young woman in the white Renault Clio wants to park her car in one of the parking spaces on the central reservation. She drives slowly in the outer lane and then suddenly turns left - just as the patrol car comes shooting out of the tunnel. Peter G. is unable to brake the Opel in time and slams into the driver's door of the Renault Clio with full force. A terrible accident that ends fatally for the young driver. She dies at the scene of the accident after rescue workers fight for her life for half an hour. Peter G. and his colleague were uninjured, apart from the passenger's broken wrist. They were taken to the Virchow Clinic of the Charité Hospital in Berlin at around 2 pm. Three hours later, they leave the hospital.

At about the same time, around half past five, Britta M. sets off for physiotherapy. Just before she pulls the apartment door shut behind her, however, she quickly types a WhatsApp message into her cell phone, addressed to her daughter Fabien: "I'm really excited to see what you've accomplished today."

Fabien wanted to open a business account at Postbank on Alexanderplatz today, because the 21-year-old is about to become the boss of a renowned café at Checkpoint Charlie. She actually didn't want to take over the store until March, but since the previous tenant was unexpectedly fired, the opportunity arose for her to turn her dream into reality earlier than planned.

However, her parents Britta and Christian are only moderately enthusiastic about the hasty plan, as Fabien wanted to take a vacation beforehand. "Say no, Fabi," her mother had admonished her. But the 21-year-old is unstoppable; she wants to work, save money, and prove herself as a leader, then take the next big step in her life in 2019: training with the Berlin police.

The fact that Fabien doesn't immediately respond to her message doesn't worry Britta; after all, she knows full well that her daughter has a lot on her plate right now.

Unsuspecting, Britta says goodbye to her husband, closes the apartment door behind her and heads for the elevator. She presses the call button and waits for the elevator to reach her floor. When the doors slide aside a moment later, two policewomen and two women from the crisis service step out of the car. They mumble a fleeting greeting to each other, and then Britta has already set foot in the empty elevator. Out of the corner of her eye, she sees that the women are aiming for her apartment.

“Excuse me, would you like to join me?”

“Are you Mrs. M?”

“Yes?”

“Can we go in for a moment?”

“What’s this about?”

“We’d like to explain that inside”.

With a sinking feeling in her stomach, Britta unlocks the apartment door and invites the officers in.

“You’re not going to tell me there’s something wrong with my daughter, are you?” asks Britta, although she thinks she already knows the answer.

“Yes, there is I’m afraid,” one of the policewomen replies, “your daughter collided with a patrol car. She didn’t survive the accident.”

Britta slumps.

“It can’t be!” roars Christian, knocking over the living room table. Plates, glasses, remote controls as well as a laptop fly across the room and fall clattering to the floor.

“Where is she? I want to see her. Now!”

“That’s not possible, Mr. M. The body has been seized.”

“It can’t be!” repeats Christian, close to tears, “You must be mistaken!”

With trembling hands, he reaches for the phone and rings all the hospitals. Soon after, however, Britta and Christian have to acknowledge the sad certainty. Their daughter is indeed dead.

The two get through the evening with nothing but tranquilizers. They constantly glance at the door, hoping to hear a key in the lock at any moment. But it remains silent - all night long.

The next morning, Britta and Christian drive to the police station to pick up Fabien's belongings. There they are informed about the details of the accident and learn that the collision apparently could have been avoided.

The day before, the first reports of the accident circulated the rumor that Fabien herself was to blame for her death. However, it is not the media from which this claim emanates, but from Peter G.'s colleagues. According to the police officers, the dead woman's smartphone was lying in the footwell. Therefore, it is assumed that the young woman had jammed her cell phone between her shoulder and head in order to make a call. Britta and Christian are horrified. Their daughter had never made a phone call while driving, they protested, and hired a lawyer.

In fact, an investigation has since been initiated against the 52-year-old chief inspector. It is assumed that G. was driving at too high a speed. Although police officers are allowed to disregard speed limits when using special rights, such as the blue light being switched on, they still have to be careful when driving on duty and ensure that no one is endangered. Section 222 of the Criminal Code states that "anyone who causes the death of a person through negligence shall be punished by imprisonment for not more than five years or by a fine."

This also applies to police officers. But was Peter G. really speeding?

An expert concludes that Fabien had not made any phone calls or sent any messages shortly before her death; a post-mortem alcohol test also comes back negative. The accident box in her car records a speed of 27 km/h at the time of the collision - so Fabien was clearly slower than the 50 km/h permitted on Grunerstrasse. Peter G. and his colleague, on the other hand, were traveling at 136 km/h on Grunerstrasse, and the speed at the time of the collision was 93 km/h, as the analysis of the data from the patrol car shows.

While the media also get wind of the investigations through this expert opinion and hotly discuss who is to blame for the accident, Peter G. keeps a low profile and does not say a single word about the fact that he collided with the car of a young woman during an emergency drive and that she died. Only a Facebook post, which the chief inspector put online a week after the accident, gives rise to speculation: "I'm so damn glad that the #policefamily can really be real. Thank you to you who are there right now, risking your ass."

When they read these words on Peter G.'s page, Fabien's parents are shaken to the core. Instead of posting a note of remorse or an apology, the police officer thanks his colleagues? What does that mean?

Britta and Christian keep scrolling. They want to find out who this man is who was driving the patrol car - and come across posts that deeply disturb them.

Peter G. seems to be a frustrated person. Frustrated by a society that pays the police too little respect and can't even behave decently during a traffic check. He blames "effeminate fellow human beings" for the overwork of the police.

"Overtime is produced more and more often by meaningless bullshit," he writes in another post on his Facebook page. And "Helpless citizens whine because they think the police have to intervene here because they don't want to get their own fingers dirty."

Peter G. is said to have told his wife that you lose if "someone is standing ten meters away from you with a knife." One should not even try to de-escalate the situation verbally, but "just pull out the gun. And shoot."

Time and again, the 52-year-old also rages against politics, which he feels has let him down. He questions the crime statistics of the Berlin police and believes that the city is capitulating to crime. Officers like him have to "work pointless overtime" and stick their necks out for a "cuddly policy". He would be too happy to use force if an arrestee provokes him. "Actually, the left is twitching right now, but we are professionals ... most of the time," he writes.

Peter G. also lives out his hobby as an avid photographer on his Facebook profile, preferring to take pictures of gloomy and morbid subjects in trendy pubs and bars. In some pictures, the chief inspector even poses himself; for one photo session, he holds a revolver to his temple, topless, with a goatee and four earrings on his left side.

In another picture, he shows himself with an axe, quoting a line from the film "Django Unchained": "War is a dirty business. I'll stick to that. Now it's going to be dirty."

G. describes his self-portraits as works of art; often puts hours into post-processing on the computer, as with the profile picture on his Facebook page, which he took on his balcony at home. He stares into the lens with an evil look, has a hood on his head and wears a long goatee. Using Photoshop, he subsequently highlighted his scrawny face, gave everything a black-and-white effect, and drew the surroundings and the background completely into black. In 2016, this picture even became a popular tattoo motif in the USA.

Peter G.'s superiors are aware of their protégé's unusual hobby but seem to turn a blind eye. They simply ask him not to "take it too far".

The longer the investigation lasts, and the more Facebook posts they read from Peter G., the more Britta and Christian M. develop a terrible suspicion: Was the chief inspector unable to control himself on January 29, 2018? Was he possibly under the influence of alcohol when he smashed into the driver's door of Fabien's Renault Clio at over 90 km/h? Their feeling tells them that something is not right.

Friends and colleagues, on the other hand, see Peter G. in a completely different light. They describe him as "a great person" - someone who is fair and has a big heart. He cares about his comrades and, if he has to, he's willing to lend a hand.

Furthermore, G. would sometimes "have a drink", sometimes even "too much to drink", but that's what many rescue workers do, especially when something bad has happened to them in the field. Blood, death, human abysses - everything that "normal citizens" don't see has to be endured by police officers. Then it sometimes happens that the chief buys them a drink. But is the chief inspector really so unscrupulous as to show up drunk for duty and thus endanger the lives of others?

In September 2018, the lawyer for the M. family is given access to the investigation file of Peter G. He notices that the last document filed away is the accident report from July 2018. According to this, nothing happened for almost one and a half months. The expert opinion, which confirms, among other things, that G. was traveling at too high a speed, is sufficient to put the chief inspector on trial - but the public prosecutor's office is not seeking a trial before the district court, but only before the traffic court in the Tiergarten district court.

The defense attorney submits a written request for a blood test and demands further investigative steps, which in his opinion are urgently necessary. A few weeks later, the public prosecutor's office explains that a blood test on Peter G. is not possible due to "legal regulations". The first indications of alcoholism had already been followed up by inquiries at the investigation office, the police department where Peter G. was employed. An alcohol test had not been carried out, as no smell of alcohol had been detected and there had been no other reason to assume that Peter G. had been drunk on duty.

More than seven months after the accident, the M. family's lawyer and the public prosecutor's office received an unexpected, anonymous tip from the Charité hospital in Berlin. There, an odor of alcohol had been detected and a blood sample had been taken from Peter G.. However, there is no proof of whether such an examination was actually carried out, because the Charité Berlin is forbidden for data protection reasons to pass on patient files of its own accord to third parties, i.e., also to the public prosecutor's office and the police.

But at the beginning of 2019, the public prosecutor's office succeeds in demanding Peter G.'s patient file via a trick: Via a court order, preliminary proceedings are initiated against hospital employees on suspicion of obstruction of justice. Officially, it is said that it is suspected that the Charité Berlin deliberately did not attach the - possibly positive - test result to Peter G.'s patient file in order "to cover up his alcoholization and to prevent him from being punished in this regard".

After the public prosecutor's office has seized and inspected Peter G.'s patient file, there can be no doubt. The test result shows a value of 1.1 blood alcohol percentage, measured one hour after the accident. It is impossible to say whether the chief inspector had been drinking immediately before going on duty or whether there was still residual alcohol in his blood from the previous evening. However, it is a fact that Peter G. was more than unfit to drive at the time of the accident. In addition to the charge of involuntary manslaughter, proceedings are now being initiated against the chief inspector for endangering road traffic through drunkenness. At the same time, he will be released from police duty with full pay - a first step towards the impending suspension.

A short time later, the media also learn of the alcohol suspicion, whereupon camera teams begin to bombard Peter G.'s apartment door in Prenzlauer Berg. The released chief inspector has no choice but to leave the city without further ado.

Before he can do that, however, he gets another visit from the police, who hold a search warrant under his nose. In the meantime, the public prosecutor's office has also become aware of the pictures on his Facebook page and accuses him of illegal possession of weapons. During the search, the police officers seize two brass knuckles, which are illegal to possess. Peter G. has to pay a fine of 1700 euros.

On October 27, 2020, the trial will begin before the extended court of lay assessors at Berlin's Tiergarten District Court. Originally, the first day of the trial was scheduled for March 17, 2020, but due to the COVID-19 pandemic, it had to be postponed.

More than two years have passed since the accident; the wounds have still not healed. Christian M. drives to the place where his daughter died almost every day; this is where he feels connected to her.

Although Christian and his wife Britta look forward to the trial with confidence and hope for a verdict in their favor, the two of them face a major setback shortly before the trial begins: Peter G.'s breathalyzer test result may not be used at the trial. A court ruled that the public prosecutor's office had obtained the file illegally. The charge of endangering road traffic by drunkenness is thus not admitted and the charge is solely negligent homicide.

Peter G. sits in a stooped position in the dock of Hall 135, while behind him the cameras of the journalists click non-stop. He wears an anthracite shirt, his gray hair short and neat. The black earrings continue to linger on his left ear, and reading glasses sit on his nose. While the press people are in the room, G. keeps his face mask on - later in the trial he will take it off.

It is the first time that the defendant faces his victims. Not only Britta and Christian M., but also Fabien herself - who smiles from a large photo in the courtroom.

Her mother has positioned the photo so that both G. and the judge can see Fabien's face clearly. The defendant should feel that he has the life of a young woman on his conscience. A young woman who was happy and still wanted to realize so many plans in her life.

After the indictment has been read out, Peter G.'s lawyer addresses Britta and Christian M. on behalf of his client. The former law enforcement officer feels "very, very close" to the terrible accident, it says. Furthermore, he is "very, very sorry" for what happened.

Christian does not believe the defendant's remorse. Almost defiantly, he raises his chin while staring at Peter G. with an expressionless gaze. He obviously wants to give the impression that the situation leaves him cold. But Christian is seething inside. Peter G. has no regrets, he says. Except perhaps that he is sitting in the dock. His wife Britta, on the other hand, is clearly grieving. She sits slumped in her chair and weeps silently into a handkerchief.

On a total of four trial days, several eyewitnesses to the accident and colleagues of the defendant are questioned. The accident report is also reviewed. The defendant himself remains silent. He had already denied guilt two years earlier in a written statement. According to this, Fabien had caused the accident by "not using the turn signal". Peter G. had assumed that he, with switched on blue light and siren, had priority. After all, he was on his way to an alleged robbery.

According to the public prosecutor's office, however, Peter G. should have expected parking lot search traffic at any time due to the parking meters on the median strip of Grunerstrasse. Due to a bend, he had also not been able to see the road properly, but had nevertheless driven out of the tunnel at over 130 km/h.

All parties involved in this process are under a lot of tension. When the fifth day of the trial was to continue on November 3, 2020, the mood finally changed. At eight o'clock in the morning, the presiding judge receives a call from the defendant, who tells him that he will not be able to attend the trial that day for health reasons. His lawyer adds that G. has a doctor's appointment at noon and will submit a corresponding certificate as soon as possible.

The judge has no choice but to postpone the hearing. A continuation without the defendant was not possible since the court could not establish an unauthorized absence.

Christian M. is outraged by the interruption. After all, he and his wife would not be asked about their state of health, even though the trial was highly emotional, especially for them.

Two years, ten months and 16 days after the accident, the verdict is decided on December 15, 2020 against the police officer Peter G. In his closing speech, the defendant's lawyer pleaded for acquittal on all counts. Fabien had changed lanes spontaneously and without signaling and may have been distracted by her cell phone. Since several witnesses testified during the trial that they had heard the siren of the patrol car loud and clear, Fabien should also have noticed the police car if she had been paying attention to the following traffic. Peter G.'s defense attorney justifies the fact that his client was driving at 130 km/h with the explanation that a police officer on duty has no time to pay attention to the speedometer and rather relies on his instinct.

The court sees this differently. "The accident could have been avoided if you had let off the gas at the tunnel exit," the judge explains, addressing the defendant.

Moreover, there was no evidence to suggest that Fabien actually typed a message into her cell phone or made a phone call shortly before she died. Every driver knows that it is initially difficult to determine where the emergency vehicle is located when an emergency siren is heard. The judge speaks of "split seconds." Even if Fabien had seen the lights of the patrol car, she could not possibly have guessed that G. and his colleague were traveling at over 130 km/h. The 21-year-old did not have the slightest chance, according to the court.

Finally, the court once again addressed the investigating authorities in clear terms, who, according to the judge, had done a "totally chaotic job". Peter G. should have been treated immediately as an accused and put into a police car. Instead, he walked freely around the scene as the person who caused the accident, while dozens of emergency personnel were there trying to save a life.

The court sentences Peter G. to fourteen months in prison, suspended. No evidence of a cover-up had been found, which means that the case with all its unanswered questions will remain largely unsolved even after the trial.

Britta and Christian, who watched the announcement of the verdict in silent tears, remain convinced that Peter G. was covered up by his colleagues. After all, how could it be that they had noticed an odor of alcohol at the Charité Berlin, but not at the scene of the accident? She had always had respect for the police, but this is now gone, Britta reports.

Nevertheless, in addition to grief and anger, the couple also experiences touching encounters. For example, when Christian recently had to call the police because a car was blocking his way. The officer recognized Christian from the media and asked him to shake his hand. He said he was incredibly sorry for what happened to Fabien.

If in most trials the verdict is the long-awaited end of a legal battle, in this case it heralds the exact opposite. The judge is sure that this debate will continue for several years, going through different instances. It is possible that another court will decide that the result of the blood test can be used after all; we will have to wait and see.

In conclusion, the judge wishes the M. family that they will finally find peace at the end of a long road and that they will eventually be able to move on with their lives. A life in which a large gap has been torn.

»For from within, out of the heart of men, proceed evil thoughts, adulteries, fornications, murders, thefts, covetousness, wickedness, deceit, lasciviousness, an evil eye, blasphemy, pride, foolishness: All these evil things come from within, and defile the man.«

- The Bible, Mark 7, 21 -

CHAPTER 3

Extra nice

Tamar S. knew that it would not go on forever. On some days she was nearly hysterical with fear; she could no longer grasp a clear thought. A feeling of panic kept rolling over her in waves. She would break out in a cold sweat and feel all her blood rush to her legs.

But now, as everything seemed to end, she felt surprisingly calm. And that's despite a flurry of flashbulbs breaking out as the police officers escort her out of her house, her hands handcuffed behind her back. The petite woman stares into dozens of television and photo cameras; numerous microphones are thrust at her. A pack of journalists shouts questions upon questions at her. But before she can think about possible answers, one of the policemen throws a gray parker over her head and leads her toward the patrol car; then he maneuvers her into the back seat behind the passenger seat. After Tamar S.'s arrest, less than 24 hours pass before what police psychologist Claudia Brockmann had predicted would happen to the special commission's investigators: Now Thomas H. will turn himself in. Now that his closest confidant can no longer be there for him.

Thomas H. was born on February 18, 1964. For his mother, he is a dream child. She loves her baby from the first second she feels the tender kicks of his little feet in her abdomen. But now, after hours of painful labor, when she can finally hold her little boy in her arms, stroke his hair and smell his skin, she feels as if her heart is about to burst with love for the little human child. Inge is completely absorbed in her role as mother. She feeds the little infant, bathes him and cuddles him; cradles her desired child in her arms while humming melodies of cheerful songs to the little boy.

The young mother reads many magazines and books about the supposedly right way to raise a child. In the smorgasbord of opinions, views and tips, the parenting guides seem to agree on one thing: the affection and attention parents show their child will be reciprocated by their offspring. But Inge soon realizes that this assumption does not apply to her little Thomas. No matter how hard she tries, no matter how much she gives him all her attention - the older the boy is, the angrier he gets. Out of nowhere, he throws screaming fits. In the process, he lashes out and kicks wildly. A harmonious and loving life together is soon no longer possible with the once desired child.

Thomas is 6 years old when his mother doesn't know what to do. She has no more ideas how to deal with her son's tantrums; how to calm him down. The boy is admitted to the psychosomatic department of the Rothenburgsort Children's Hospital. After several examinations and assessments of their little patient's behavior, the doctors come to their conclusion: the child is suffering from a neurotic disorder caused by his mother's educational insecurities. In order to control his outbursts of rage, the doctors give the boy strong psychotropic drugs to calm him down.

But the tranquilizers have no effect on Thomas' fits of raving madness. Just as little as his family's household goods. During his fits of rage, Thomas destroys furniture and other objects. One day, his desperate mother's hand slips and the boy receives a slap in the face. His reaction is to be remembered by Inge: The boy hurls his mother against a wall in an explosion of violence, breaking her wrist. Then he spits a "You'll never hit me again without listening to me first!" at her.

The first time Thomas feels an inner urge to kill, he is 10 years old. Over and over again, the same scene plays out in the child's mind's eye. How he goes into the kitchen and takes one of the large carving knives from the cutlery drawer into his small hand. How he looks at the long blade of the knife and watches his reflection in the brightly polished steel. His fist closes tighter and tighter around the handle of the cutting tool until his knuckles turn all white. Then he imagines that the pretty neighbor is standing in front of him and that he is ramming the carving knife deep into her body. In his mind's eye, he sees the incredulous look on the woman's face as he pulls the bloodied knife out of her body, only to plunge it directly back into her stomach. He can literally feel her warm blood running down his arm. But it will still take time for Thomas to turn his killing fantasies into reality.

In the years to come, Thomas H. is always surprised by the desire to kill a woman. From one second to the next it overtakes him - this irrepressible compulsion to kill. One evening, after he has prepared and eaten a warm meal, the young man sets about washing the dishes. Suddenly, he drops the dish sponge into the sink with the hot water and dirty dishes and storms out of the house. Greedily, he drives up and down the streets in the darkness of the night. Thomas H. is on the lookout for a suitable victim to take his life. His eyes restlessly search the sidewalks. But on this evening no woman is walking lonely and alone. Unfulfilled, he drives back home. And continues to do the dishes.

At the age of 23, the trained graphic designer succeeds in getting hold of a woman for the first time. It is November 23, 1987, when the young man is again overcome by the urge to kill. Again, he gets into his car and drives aimlessly through Hamburg-Rissen. Out of the corner of his eye, he sees a young woman walking along the side of the road. She immediately attracts his attention. Her name is Luisa K. and she just arrived in Rissen by S-Bahn. The 20-year-old lives here with her parents. But on this evening, the student is not on her way home. She has an appointment with a friend to play squash together.

The man turns his car around, switches off the headlights and turns into a side street. He grabs the knife that is lying ready next to him on the passenger seat. At knifepoint, he forces the young woman, who has no chance, to get into his car. Intimidated, she does not defend herself against her tormentor. He then drives her to his rented apartment, which is on the top floor of an apartment building. When the student is forced to enter the apartment, romantic music is playing from a clock radio and the bedroom is lit by candlelight. Thomas H. will later claim that he made his apartment "really cozy". An inner struggle had been raging inside him. It was the compulsion to kill against his conscience. "I couldn't stop it. I knew she was going to die, that was the option. I had to do it. When it's over, I'll be Thomas H. again." That evening, the landlady in the basement gets nothing of the agony that Luisa endures one floor above her.

After the graphic artist rapes the young woman, he kneels down next to his terrified victim, strokes her hair, kisses her cheek and forehead, and whispers "Bye" to her before strangling the young woman with a cable. Unnoticed, the murderer manages to get the student's body out of the apartment. Two days after her murder, workers accidentally discover Luisa K.'s body near Kaltenkirchen.

Only six weeks later, in January 1988, Thomas H. meets a 19-year-old student in Hamburg-Wandsbek in the early evening. He pursues the high school student until he is close behind her. Then he holds a knife to her neck. To show the girl that he means business, he carves into her skin. Then the graphic artist forces her to come with him. After the student gets over the initial paralyzing shock, her will to survive kicks in. With trembling knees, she tears herself away, tries to run away and screams for help. But no one hears her desperate cries. Thomas H. quickly catches up with his victim after only a few meters. He gets hold of the back of her jacket and grabs hold of it. The young woman tries to tear herself away, slips out of her jacket, falls, gets up and runs for her life again. But again, he manages to catch up with her after a few steps. He reaches out and holds the student by her sweater. Again, he presses the sharp blade of the knife firmly against her neck, the other hand he presses over her mouth to prevent her from screaming. The high school student surrenders: the fear is too great that the attacker could hurt her again with the knife. Thomas H. also forces her into the house where he lives. The girl still tries to push her foot between the door and the hinge to prevent the unknown man from closing the front door. In vain. The student realizes the hopelessness of her situation. In a split second, it flashes through her mind that only prudence can help her now. She decides not to provoke her attacker and comply with his demands.

The young girl tries to establish a conversation with the man. "What are you going to do with me?" she asks him anxiously, almost in a whisper. Her voice threatens to break. But the man does not answer her. Instead, he fetches two bathrobe belts. He instructs the student to lie on her stomach on the floor in the living room. Then he ties her hands behind her back with a belt. "What are you doing to me?" the girl asks him again. "I want to fuck you," he murmurs to her before stuffing a gag so deep into her mouth that her tongue frenulum tears, and a bleeding wound appears. Then he pulls down her pants and rapes his victim. The high school student's cheek rubs across the bristly carpet as she repeatedly feels this stabbing pain in her abdomen. In agony, she tries to scream, but no sound leaves her gagged mouth. Today is the day she will die; the girl is sure of it. The student is more perplexed when Thomas H. rolls off her in satisfaction and loosens her bonds. He also takes the gag out of her mouth - and lets her go. The 19-year-old can hardly believe her luck to still be alive. She immediately files a complaint against her rapist, but it is still several months before the trial, which the perpetrator spends in freedom. This is a circumstance that costs the life of another woman.

It is February 11, 1988, when Thomas H. goes hunting again. He is driving along a lonely road at night when he sees a woman walking along the side of the road. The 29-year-old Paula S. had attended an event that evening and is now on her way home on foot when suddenly a car pulls up next to her. A man gets out and stands directly in front of her. In his hand she sees the blade of a knife flashing in the moonlight. Thomas H. forces the mother of two to get into his car. He takes the young woman to his apartment. Once there, he ties his terrified victim to the bed. The woman killer rapes and mutilates his victim with a knife. In the process, he tortures and burns her skin with cigarette butts. After hours of martyrdom, he puts his hands around the mother's neck and squeezes tightly until he can no longer detect any movement in his victim. Even now, he manages to get the woman's naked corpse out of his apartment unobserved. He dumps the dead Paula S. in a field near Bargfeld-Stegen, where she is found a few days later.

In May 1988, the trial of Thomas H. for the rape of the 19-year-old schoolgirl takes place at the district court in Hamburg-Wandsbek. He himself remains silent on the charges. The 24-year-old defendant receives a prison sentence of 18 months for coercion, deprivation of liberty, and bodily harm. He is not held accountable for the rape. The chairman of the criminal proceedings states in his verdict: “It may be doubtful in the legal sense whether the witness voluntarily gave herself up to sexual intercourse or was forced to do so by the continuing violence of the preceding events. However, the defendant must be believed, or at least cannot be disproved, that in his delusion he sincerely meant that the witness sympathized with him and wanted to perform intercourse with him of her own free will.”

Two years pass before Thomas H. commits the third murder that makes him a serial killer according to the common definition. The 22-year-old cosmetics student Anika T. falls victim to him on November 27, 1990, barely a year after his release from prison. She missed her train and is now on her way home on foot. “I immediately hit the brakes,” says H. Then, he says, he offered the young woman a ride. “She was incredibly trusting” and had accepted his offer with thanks. As the two then talked about dogs in the car, he was suddenly overcome again by the urge to kill. Inwardly fighting against this urge to kill, he is gripped by an inconceivable rage because the cosmetics student does not notice the fight he is currently fighting. “She should have seen that, but she was babbling naively. I knew I was going to kill her. I didn't have access to myself anymore.” He takes her to his weekend home in Holm-Seppensen. Here he tortures, rapes, and strangles the young woman. When the 22-year-old is dead, he gets a red dog blanket, a hatchet as well as a saw, and begins to mutilate the hands of the killed. Five days after the murder, the victim is found by a walker in a wooded area in the municipality of Holm-Seppensen. In addition to the strangulation marks, forensic experts find that the fingers of her left hand have been amputated; her right hand has been completely severed. In addition, the murderer severely mutilated Anika T.'s left eye.

Some criminal investigators later think, in reference to the mutilations, that the destruction of Anika's left eye could be related to Thomas H.'s girlfriend at the time - because she is cross-eyed on the left. It seems that he wanted to transfer this characteristic to his victim. Thomas' relationship is already in crisis at this point. By mutilating her hands, he possibly wanted to make the identification of Anika more difficult. On October 7, 1989, a 31-year-old female jogger was murdered in a forest in Buchholz. A short time later, a 38-year-old man took his own life. His partner at the time reported to the police; she could not explain why her partner had committed suicide. According to media reports, a DNA sample of the man was then routinely taken and compared with the skin particles found under the fingernails of the killed jogger. And: hit! The man who committed suicide was the murderer of the 31-year-old woman. This fact was also reported in the newspapers, on the radio and on television.

It can be assumed that Thomas H. was aware of this reporting since he was living in Nordheide at the time. It is possible that Anika T. scratched her attacker while she was defending herself against her tormentor and that Thomas H. mutilated her hands in order not to be convicted as a murderer possibly also via his DNA under her fingernails.

In all three women killed by Thomas H., the forensic experts documented injuries caused by blunt external force and injuries in the genital area caused by sexual acts. Traces of sperm were also found on the victims' bodies. But that's not all: the woman killer, in order to torture his victims and make them compliant, also inflicted injuries on them with needles, knives, and a hatchet. He mutilates the women, cuts off their fingers and cuts out sections of skin from their bodies. In some cases, he inflicts these massive injuries while his victims are still alive. In the media and in court, the bodies of the murdered victims are later described as "horribly" and "gruesomely" dressed.

During the investigation of the case of the killed cosmetics student Anika T., Thomas H. is targeted by the criminal investigators for the first time. His previous conviction for coercion, deprivation of liberty and bodily harm to the 19-year-old schoolgirl in Hamburg-Wandsbek in 1988 now prompts the officers to investigate the convicted man. They discover parallels between the rape of the high school student and the murder of Anika T.

Hans-Peter Kröger, a member of the homicide squad, is one of those detectives who ring Thomas H.'s doorbell on Christmas Eve in 1990 to confront him with their suspicions. Kröger recounts: "He seemed very calm to me [...] At first I didn't have the impression that he was the murderer of Anika T. He seemed sporty and attractive. He seemed sporty-attractive and safe. Then I talked to my older colleague who said that this was our man - he was shaking all over." And his older colleague was to be proved right. The suspect is brought to the police station for questioning.

At first, Thomas H. still seemed harmless to homicide investigator Kröger, until the officer was taught better. He will later state for the record: "At the time [...] he made a rather naïve, somewhat childlike impression. I had the feeling that not a single drop of water could cloud him. Later, when we questioned him, one had to get the impression that he knew exactly what he was doing." Thomas H. cries during questioning and seems remorseful. Detectives are therefore hoping that their suspect will soon make a confession and finally admit to having killed Anika T. "He kept saying, 'I've got it in my stomach, but I can't get it into my head, and I can't express it like that,'" the criminal investigator will later recount. When the accused appears to Kroeger as if he is about to give in and he feels he has a good connection to the crime suspect, he asks his colleague to leave him alone with Thomas H. in the interrogation room. Kröger's colleague complies with the request. Thomas H. later takes advantage of this situation to claim that Kroeger had beaten him to force a confession.

Criminal proceedings are initiated against the detective, which continue until the end of the murder trial. Only then can the suspicion against Kröger of having mistreated the perpetrator be dispelled. But it's a long road until then, and the criminal investigator is constantly hovering in fear that he could lose his job. "In the end, the truth did come out. I didn't hit him. He had made it all up so as to be able to recant his statement or confession," Kröger sums up.

Despite the serious accusations made by Thomas H. against the police officer, the trial of 28-year-old H. took place in May 1992 at the Stade Regional Court. The forensic team had found pieces of clothing belonging to the killed Anika T. on the suspect's person. They secured a total of 1500 traces. Trace No. 456a is a microscopic red fiber bundle. The same fibers were also discovered in a long bone of a severed finger of the victim. During the trial, a psychiatric expert described that the defendant's motive may have been a "narcissistic self-esteem crisis." Meanwhile, the defendant is christened "Heidemörder" (heath killer) by the tabloid press, in reference to the places where he committed his acts. The court convicts Thomas H. of coercion and manslaughter. In the case of Anika T., who was killed, the court also does not assume that she was raped. The presiding judge justifies this by saying that the victim "endured the sex in order to prevent something worse". He assumes that the defendant threatened his victim massively beforehand. "A gas gun, knives and scalpels were present as tools," the chairman said. Then, the judge assumes, Thomas H. realized after the crime that "he had messed up his life." However, he does not recognize murder characteristics. The court sentences Thomas H. to 12 years in prison.

This sentence is overturned by the Federal Court of Justice following an appeal by the responsible public prosecutor. In January 1993, Thomas H. is now sentenced to 14 years' imprisonment for murder in combination with rape, and placement in a psychiatric ward is ordered.

By the time the Federal Court of Justice overturns the sentence against Thomas H., the criminal investigators have gathered enough circumstantial evidence linking H. also to the murders of Luisa K. and Paula S. that the public prosecutor's office again brings charges against the man. This time for double murder. The trial is again taking place at the Stade Regional Court. According to the accusation, the defendant is said to have treacherously murdered the two women to satisfy his sex drive and to cover up a crime. H. himself does not seem particularly distressed by the accusations. His thin mouth even hints at a smile during the trial. Tension or remorse cannot be read from his face or posture. Outwardly, the Heath Killer remains cold and unaffected during the trial. Even during the gruesome details of the murders, which are described in all their particulars during the trial, he does not make a face. In this trial, too, the defendant remains silent about the accusations.

The parents of Luisa K. do not manage to follow the trial of their daughter's murderer in the courtroom. The wounds inflicted on them by the loss of their child are too deep. They can't bear to be in the same room with their Luisa's murderer and breathe the same air as him. But they find the strength to write a letter that is read during the trial of Thomas H. It is an expression of their pain over the loss of their child. It is an expression of their pain at the loss and their anger at their daughter's killer. They admonish the court and the public that "it is always the perpetrator who is the focus of attention and interest. The victim, however, often exists only in the files, and there is a danger that he or she will lead only a shadowy existence in the literal sense. The fact that this victim was once a young, lively human child, who stood on the threshold of adulthood with a hopeful future, as a 20-year-old woman knowing that life was still ahead of her, is all too easily forgotten in the sober facts." They let read further: "And still something runs the risk to fall behind. Every victim leaves behind numerous survivors. Parents, grandparents, siblings, friends - people who loved and cherished. Each and every one of these people has not only lost something irretrievable, not only has something been taken from them forever, but a part of their own life story, their own past as well as their future, has died with our daughter. A part of one's own soul has been extinguished, yes, one can say, a part of one's own self has also been murdered. Seen in this way, the murder is added to the sum of all partial murders of people they loved. Seen through such eyes, each murder almost amounts to a double murder." The words of the parents seem to leave the accused completely cold. The 28-year-old's pale face is completely frozen.

During the trial, a psychiatric expert discusses Thomas H.'s behavior. He reacted "mask-like" when he was in trouble. Even when the serial killer confesses to the expert after 15 days of trial that he committed the murders, he comes across to the expert as an empathy-less, cold robot. As if he were explaining to the psychiatrist how best to bake a cake. No sign of remorse, shame, compassion, or horror can be read on the serial killer's face as he recounts his deeds in all their horror. The Heath murderer himself believes that he was " extra nice " to his victims. The expert asks the defendant whether he was able to sleep after his first murder of Luisa K. "Of course, I could sleep. Everything was tidy," he answers, almost with incomprehension in his voice at the psychiatrist's question. Regarding the murder of the mother of two, Paula S., the doctor asks Thomas H. what the woman must have felt while he tortured her for hours. "It certainly wasn't nice for her," he answers coolly. After the expert has analyzed the biography and the behavior of the accused in detail, he concludes that in the further development of the youth "severe neurotic disorders under the aspect of permanent narcissistic tensions" had led to the murders of the young women. He attests him a high probability of recidivism with an undiminished urge to kill.

When the verdict is pronounced, the Heath murderer shows no emotion. The court considers the rare murder characteristic of homicidal desire to have been realized and sentences the defendant in this trial to a total term of life imprisonment. The court also decides once again to commit him to a psychiatric institution. In his explanation of the sentence, the presiding judge insistently points out that he does not believe Thomas H.'s descriptions. The women certainly did not go along with him of their own free will and voluntarily had sexual intercourse with him. All three victims were "helplessly at the mercy" of the murderer.

Thomas H. is sent to the Ochsenzoll psychiatric hospital. However, the murderer proves to be a recalcitrant patient. The head of the house at the time recounts: "He was constantly trying to make it clear to the staff where his rights lay, and if he couldn't assert them in a normal conversation - this involved everything from the choice of food to having his own computer - he immediately took legal action and instrumentalized his entire environment so that it was not only forced to answer to him, but also to deal with his lawyers. He never, at any time, let up."

The convicted serial killer is supposed to undergo therapy at the Ochsenzoll Forensic Center, but he refuses. The usual therapeutic approaches would not do justice to his complex personality. After all, he is no ordinary serial killer; he suffers from a multiple personality disorder. But the experts' verdict is clear: Nothing about their patient's behavior indicates that he suffers from this psychiatric disorder. The doctors in Ochsenzoll write Thomas H. off as therapy-resistant. They have no choice because the convicted woman killer refuses any therapeutic measures. So, the days pass by in the mental hospital for the Heath murderer. That is until the psychologist Tamar S. starts her work in Ochsenzoll in July 1994, four weeks after the woman killer moved into house 18.

Tamar S. was born in Israel in 1957. Her father is a respected doctor. Her mother is a Hungarian Jew who survived the concentration camp Theresienstadt. Tamar is just 16 years old when her mother dies of cancer.

The young girl discovers her homosexuality at an early age. She becomes a co-founder of the Israeli homosexual movement. Here she meets a German woman with whom she falls in love. She follows her great love to Germany. To obtain permanent residency rights here, she marries a man as a pretense.

Tamar S. begins to study. She studies American studies, English studies, German studies as well as philosophy and graduates with a master's degree. But her thirst for knowledge is far from quenched: she also begins to study psychology and criminology. It is April 1993 when the 36-year-old begins her one-year internship in forensic psychiatry at the general hospital in Hamburg-Ochsenzoll. After completing her internship, Tamar S. was offered a half-time position as an occupational therapist in House 18 of the forensic department in August 1994. This is where the notorious Heath murderer is housed. She accepts.

The occupational therapist does not receive much recognition from her colleagues. Some of them consider her unprofessional. She sometimes reacts too emotionally to the patients; she is unable to maintain a professional distance. This is also the case with the Heath murderer: she cooks, paints, and plays music with him. At some point, he calls Tamar S. just "my little one". Even though the lack of distance from her clients is not well received by her colleagues, they appreciate Tamar S. for her tireless commitment, for example. Although she has a half-time position in the clinic, she usually stays in House 18 for the entire workday, attending all rounds and meetings. Other employees later state that they perceived their colleague as "increasingly dissatisfied."

What follows will leave many observers as well as members of the media shaking their heads and will briefly put Tamar on the front pages throughout Germany. The events seem as if two life stories were interlocking like puzzle pieces: Tamar S., a psychologist who is no longer quite young and who cannot fully realize her actual potential in her part-time position, meets a known rapist and serial killer - her greatest possible challenge. She becomes convinced that she can help Thomas H. and “cure” him. This is what he persuades her to do: only she would understand him; only she could help him. The psychologist literally throws herself at the patient. The wife killer meanwhile assumes that 12 children live in his body. They control him. And they are also responsible for the terrible deeds he has committed. Only when these evil creatures in him are eradicated, he is cured and can live in freedom again. Even though the other specialists continue to doubt this self-diagnosis, psychologist Tamar S. shows understanding for the serial killer and his situation. When she fully supports the self-diagnosis of Thomas H.’s multiple personality in front of her colleagues, she is laughed at. This reaction causes something disastrous, which makes the two people, who met by chance, practically become one: Two marginalized people, a psychologist who is not taken seriously and her imprisoned patient, fight from now on against the rest of the world.

Thomas H. takes advantage of the nature of his occupational therapist. He is perceived by many people, especially women, as a likeable and charming man who has something winning about him. The former head of the house in the prison for inmates with special needs says about the wife-killer: "Thomas H. appears outwardly charming, intelligent, very eager to please. However, this façade quickly crumbles - the moment you deny him something, Thomas H. emerges as the person he was and is in my eyes. Namely as someone who is all about exercising power, and if somehow possible violence, over others. A beast, even though I hate to say that about a human being."

It is September 1, 1995, when Tamar S. rents a one-room apartment in the Hamburg-Hohenfelde district under a false identity. She then withdraws a considerable sum of DM 250,000 (approx. 125,000 euros) from her account. An inheritance has helped her to this wealth. Only a short time after she has done these things, Tamar is told that she is to be transferred to another department because of conflicts in her work environment, including with her superiors. This would mean that she would not be able to work with Thomas H. any time soon.

But the psychologist and her client have long since come up with a plan. The fact that Tamar S. is now to be transferred only means that they will have to implement it sooner than expected. The therapist wants to help her patient - the convicted wife-killer who has been predicted to have a high probability of recidivism and is considered untreatable.

It is the afternoon of September 27 when Tamar S. takes the convicted serial killer out of his cell. She passes through security gates and bulletproof glass doors with him until they enter the gym. After Thomas H. breaks a hole through the boarding, he reaches the roof of the building, from where he rappels down to freedom. Undiscovered, the fugitive takes the subway to the apartment he rented under a false name, where he hides for the next few weeks. Only a few streets away from police station 31 in Hamburg-Hohenfelde.

Immediately after Thomas H.'s escape is noticed, a huge police apparatus is set in motion. The pressure to find the serial killer quickly and render him harmless is enormous. The manhunt for the escaped convict runs around the clock. Approximately 250 people who were in contact with the escaped convict are being checked by investigators according to a specific grid. It is clear to the investigators that Tamar S. played a key role in the escape of Thomas H. However, she is not the only one who is believed to have helped the woman killer; rather, it is assumed that there was an environment of helpers. For example, the Hamburg lawyer Martin S., who has already been convicted of fraud, is suspected. Thomas H. had met him during his pre-trial detention. Everyone in the helper environment seems to be aware of the surveillance by the police. No one contacts the escaped criminal.

The special commission wants to outwit the helpers with a trick and thus find out where H. is hiding. For a long time, it is denied that this " trick " existed, because the line between legal and illegal is very thin. After the whole thing is over, criminal investigator Reinhard Chedor tells NDR 1 Niedersachsen: "When we were relatively sure which people could be considered for organizing the escape, we produced a letter - an extortion letter." In their fictitious letter, the investigators write that the author knew exactly that the addressees were responsible for Thomas H.'s escape. Then, to tighten the proverbial thumbscrews even more, the "blackmailer" demands a large cash sum for his silence. As ingenious as this coup is, it is with a little disappointment that Chedor admits that this letter did lead to those involved in the helper's environment talking about the escaped criminal on the tapped telephone; however, not a word was said about where Thomas H. was hiding. Chedor does not want to go any further into the investigative hit. Even if the blackmail letter does not bring the desired success, the behavior of Tamar S. confirms what the investigators suspected all along. She knows something and she supports the fugitive. It was now time for the next blow: on December 30,

1995, police officers arrested the psychologist in front of her apartment door, amidst a huge press hype. The media representatives, however, are not there purely by chance and document the arrest of Tamar S. - the reporters have been briefed beforehand by the special commission. In any case, the investigators want Thomas H. to know that his closest confidant and helper is now no longer available to him.

Claudia Brock, police psychologist of the special commission analyzes that the serial killer must have had contact with his helpers for a long time due to his prison conditions and "against the background of his need for uniqueness, but also his distrust of other people". In addition, he must have been sure that his confidants also had the logistical prerequisites for an escape: for example, a place to live and cash. Thomas H. cannot earn his own living, because to do so he would have to leave his cover and would be exposed. Tamar S. fulfilled all these conditions: She possessed the keys to open the doors to freedom for him, she had a considerable inheritance, and she too was convinced that Thomas H. was not properly housed at the Ochsenzoll Clinic. Tamar S. believes, like the Heath killer, that he can be helped and regain his freedom, if only he were offered the right therapy. It is Claudia Brockmann who advises the investigators to adopt the strategy of arresting Tamar S. with a great media hype. As soon as the escaped criminal hears about it, he would turn himself in, because then all his prerequisites for a successful escape would be gone. And Brockmann predicts that after his failed escape from the psychiatric hospital, the Heath killer will need to make a grand entrance according to the motto "Here I am".

On New Year's Eve 1995, a fat, balding man, who has just stuffed a handful of valerian tablets into his mouth to calm himself down, enters the police station in Hamburg-Hohenfelde. The 32-year-old in a blue tracksuit is carrying a plastic bag. The police officer on duty looks at his counterpart somewhat perplexed when he claims that he is the wanted Thomas H. "He looks so very different from the pictures that have been going through the press for weeks of the fugitive criminal," runs through the officer's head. But his doubts are blown away when the chubby man lets the police officer look inside the plastic bag he brought with him: it is filled to halfway with banknotes; the remaining sum of Tamar's 250,000 DM. The officer lifts his gaze from the bag and now looks deeply into the eyes of his counterpart, whose mouth twists into a mischievous smile. At this moment, an ice-cold shiver runs down the policeman's spine. The wanted serial killer is actually standing in front of him.

As predicted, the Heath killer claims that he did not turn himself in because his supporter was arrested. It had been planned from the beginning that he would end his escape himself. With this action, he only wanted to draw attention to the deplorable conditions in the Ochsenzoll detention center. But the detectives found out that Thomas H. and Tamar S. had planned to flee to Israel, the psychologist's home country. Back in house 18, extensive security measures are taken to prevent the serial killer from escaping again at all costs. Thomas H. is given a single room so that he has no contact with his fellow inmates. He is also alone during his daily walk around the yard, which requires that all other inmates be locked up before Thomas H. is allowed out into the fresh air. The staff taking care of the escapee is selected with great care by the warden - they must be "without fault or blame." In addition to being housed individually, the woman killer is monitored day and night. His room is thoroughly searched on a regular basis. Thomas H. is anything but enthusiastic about the way he is treated. He threatens the house director to kill her if he is ever released.

Tamar S. is sentenced by a court to two and a half years' probation for aiding and abetting the escape after the Heath killer is arrested again. Other people who were suspected of being part of the helpers' circle were not prosecuted because they had not helped Thomas H. in the actual escape operation.

To everyone's surprise and to the displeasure of the institutions, the psychologist, despite her original homosexual orientation, marries her patient in March 1997. Since the clinic management in Ochsenzoll had banned her former employee Tamar S. from the clinic and only lifted the ban later, Thomas H. must be taken to a Hamburg remand prison on March 13 under the utmost security precautions. Here, a registrar performs the marriage ceremony between the woman killer and the psychologist. There are no wedding festivities. Immediately after the wedding ceremony, Thomas S., as he is now called, is taken back to the psychiatric ward.

Claudia Brockmann later says that everyone involved was very surprised when the Heath killer wanted to marry his psychologist, against all odds. But she assumes that one of the main reasons for the marriage - from Thomas H.'s side - was Tamar S.'s considerable inheritance. Brockmann also believes it is conceivable that Tamar S., on the other hand, agreed to the marriage so that Thomas H. could change his last name to that of his new wife.

Tamar S. denies this: she loves Thomas H. and has felt sorry for him since their first meeting. He was not a murderer. Since he is ill, he cannot bear any responsibility for his actions. The two had never met erotically; the situation was too tense during the escape of the woman killer from Ochsenzoll. She was also surprised about the change in her sexual orientation, she calls it a "physical and emotional revolution". Even though Tamar S. is aware that the two of them "may not experience a married life like others," she would be willing to give up everything for the relationship with her husband, the convicted woman killer.

Police psychologist Claudia Brockmann reveals to the public that the serial killer is rarely polite, let alone friendly, to his wife. If she does something wrong in his eyes, he attacks her verbally; not infrequently, he even calls her a "stupid cow." The supervisory staff has often said that they do not like to supervise Tamar S.'s visits to her husband because it "sucks" to listen to how he treats his wife.

It is 2003 when Thomas S. files a complaint with the Hamburg Regional Court. The murderer is demanding relief in his detention center, and he wants to meet with his wife unsupervised in one of the visitors' rooms. However, the Ochsenzoll Clinic does not comply with his demands; the danger to life and limb of Tamar S. is too great. The regional court thus decisively rejects the criminal's complaint. To date, the serial killer's marriage to his therapist has not been consummated; they are only allowed to see each other under supervision. Tamar S. lives alone and penniless in Hamburg. She still stands by her husband Thomas H. and visits him regularly in the Ochsenzoll psychiatric hospital.

The action to enforce the marriage is the last time Thomas H. has made the headlines. Since then, it has been quiet around the Heath killer. Only for the criminal investigator Hans Peter Kroeger it is certain that one will hear something from the woman murderer again sometime: “It was always his thing to be in the headlines, whether it was about the arrest at that time or about the trial. He was always in the media.” Kröger is sure that Thomas H. will eventually do something again to shock the public and get attention. The main thing is that he is in the spotlight.

The names of the victims have been changed for their sake and for the protection of the bereaved families.

One thief calls the other a rogue.

- German proverb -

CHAPTER 4

A game of cat and mouse

A clear spring night in May 1988 in Berlin. A deafening bang shatters the silence of the night and startles the residents out of their sleep. A homemade bomb detonates in the men's department of the famous luxury department store KaDeWe on Wittenbergplatz. A few minutes later, dozens of police cars and fire engines with their sirens blaring race through Schöneberg to the scene. The emergency forces are confronted with a picture of devastation. The force of the detonation causes property damage of DM 250,000 (around 130.000 USD).

Fortunately, no one is injured in the attack, but this relief is soon followed by another shock. The management receives a blackmail letter from the bomber. He wants DM 500,000 (around 260.000 USD) from the Group. If they do not respond to his demands, further attacks will follow and for each death the amount will increase by another million, he writes. The money package is to be thrown from a moving train on his command. The management fears that employees or customers could be injured or even killed if they do not respond to the extortionist's demand. They procure the half million DM and carefully package the money. They are supported in their plan by the Berlin police.

On the day the money is to be handed over, the blackmailer contacts the police by radio: "Take the train at 8:43 p.m. in the direction of Frohnau. You take the last carriage and stand on the right-hand side as seen in the direction of travel," the blackmailer instructs them in a calm voice. Not a trace of excitement can be heard. Along the railroad track and in the train cars, many civilian police officers have taken up positions, ready to open the chase for the perpetrator as soon as he grabs the money package. The train continues to pick up speed as the perpetrator radioed in again. "Attention, this is the blackmailer! Throw the money out now! Throw the money out NOW!" it buzzes through the radio. The tension in the man's voice is now clearly audible after all. The officer takes the wrapped money package and does as he is told. He lets the extortion money fall out through the open upper window of the train compartment.

From the dense undergrowth along the train track, the money messenger is observed by the perpetrator. When he hears the money package hit the ground, he leaves his cover. He only glances at the departing train before grabbing the bundle of money and disappearing into the darkness of the night. All this happens so quickly that none of the police officers manages to pursue him after the train comes to a halt due to an emergency stop.

Gasping, the blackmailer then runs into the nearby industrial area shaking with exertion and excitement. His path leads him to a car repair shop where he works as an employee. Here he plans to hide himself and his loot until the police give up looking for him and leave. On the way to his hiding place, the small figure with the money package in his hand is seen by two teenagers who take advantage of the seclusion and quiet of the industrial area to practice new tricks with their skateboards. The next day, based on their observations, a police sketch artist draws the face of the perpetrator who, the previous night, has ushered in the most spectacular series of extortions in German criminal history.

On March 14, 1950, little Arno Funke was born out of wedlock in West Berlin. His mother comes from Norway, which is why Arno develops a special relationship to the Scandinavian country with its high mountains, snow-covered glaciers, and numerous coastal fjords during his life. His father, a native Berliner, leaves the family when his young son is six years old. Until then, Arno grows up in Berlin's Neukölln district of Rudow in a cozy wooden cottage with a large, overgrown garden where the little boy can let off steam. From now on, it's up to the single mother to make a living. Even though she doesn't have it easy; she puts up a brave fight. She and her son move into an apartment in an apartment building in Berlin-Neukölln.

In April 1956, the Funke offspring starts school at the Matthias Claudius Primary School in Rudow. The child with the irrepressible play instinct finds his time at school a torture. Soon Arno loses his joy and desire to learn. The teachers' beatings drive the last motivation to learn out of him. Only in art and sports does the student get a "very good" on his report card, otherwise Arno impresses only with poor grades. Although the boy is quite intelligent and enthusiastic about many things. Later, in a test without speech, he is given an IQ of 145. Arno is thus considered highly gifted and plays, for example, in the same league as the 37th President of the United States, Richard Nixon, who was certified to have an IQ of 143.

For Christmas, the little boy is given the experiment kit "The Little Radio Man". At first, Arno is occupied with electronics until "The Little Chemist" is placed under the Christmas tree at the next Christmas. With this chemistry experiment kit, he also makes his first experiments with the highly explosive black powder. Arno is very inventive; he makes telescopes and microscopes out of his father's old glasses and magnifying glasses. The jack-of-all-trades also enjoys photography and making his own pictures. When Arno is older, he spends most of his free time at the local library. He devours tomes on astronomy and physics; for distraction, he immerses himself in tales of Greek myths.

Arno is fourteen years old when his parents get back together. His mother still keeps the apartment in Berlin-Neukölln, but she moves her son back in with his father. The teenager is happy about the reconciliation, especially because he now lives again in the quaint wooden house with the spacious garden plot. Here he has his peace and quiet; he can tinker and experiment undisturbed.

Arno spends the last school year 1964/65 at the Rütli School in Neukölln. The teachers he meets here manage the seemingly impossible: the truant officer discovers his desire to learn the school material. His grades improve from one moment to the next, and within a very short time the boy is at the top of his class. The school staff is enthusiastic about the change in the former problem pupil. But he has no intention of attending school any longer than necessary. Arno is no longer in the mood. He is tempted by the supposed freedom of adults. All the good coaxing from the teachers doesn't help.

At first, Funke starts an apprenticeship as an office clerk. But it only takes three months before the apprentice realizes that this is not his dream job. He breaks off the training. A photographer's apprenticeship follows, but here the master trainer terminates the training relationship. The young man was not suitable enough for the job. An apprenticeship as a sign and advertising manufacturer follows, which Arno successfully completes.

It is 1970 when Funke Senior dies at the age of 72. The 20-year-old, who was born out of wedlock, and his mother have no claim to the deceased's inheritance. They lose the cozy wooden house and garden to their legal heirs. A heavy blow in addition to the grief over the loss of their father.

Six months after the funeral, Arno Funke leaves Berlin. He travels all over Germany. From Passau to Starnberg, from Schorndorf to Meppen, from Ansbach to Dortmund. While he moves around, he earns his living as a disc jockey. The young man feels at home in the North Rhine-Westphalian city of Bielefeld. The following two years Arno works for a large beverage company. He quickly settles into his new adopted city and meets a young woman. Marriage follows and a move to Berlin. However, the marriage is short-lived and is soon divorced again.

After the separation in 1973, Arno moves in with his mother, who has gone back to her native Haugesund in Norway after the death of her father and lives there with her new partner. Funke enjoys the beauty of the Scandinavian country with its untouched nature. He earns his living as a construction worker.

However, his love for a pretty young woman draws him back to Berlin after a short time. After his return, Arno works in his learned profession as a sign and advertising manufacturer. His work involves handling all kinds of paints and solvents. A circumstance that later causes him to become seriously ill with nervous disorders. After six years, the young couple went their separate ways again. The 29-year-old now turns his life upside down once again and takes a risk: he becomes self-employed in 1979. Instead of designing advertising and billboards, the artistically gifted Funke now decorates the bodies of cars and motorcycles in a car repair shop. He designs colorful images, which he then applies to his customers' vehicles using paint and special-effect paints. Inevitably, the young man now inhales more solvents even more intensively, which continuously damage his nerves further.

Then Arno meets and falls in love with a young Korean woman. The couple goes through seven emotional years. "[She] robbed me of part of my mind, the other part dissolved in solvent vapors," Arno Funke sums up. From now on, the thirty-year-old severely suffers from depression. He feels an inner emptiness; it seems as if there is no longer any joy or meaning in his life. No matter how hard he fights his inner demons, he can't fight them. His mind seems to be packed in absorbent cotton, in which his thoughts circle. "You are worthless!", "You are useless!", "The world wouldn't be worse without you!", "Nobody needs you!", it goes through his head incessantly. To escape from his thoughts, Funke numbs himself with alcohol. But he can't overcome the evil spirit of depression with it. Finally, in addition to self-doubt and suicidal thoughts, there is also the perpetual lack of money. He makes a living every month, but he is unable to take a vacation, relax, or treat himself to something, despite his self-employment as a car sprayer. This is an explosive mixture, in the truest sense of the word, that soon keeps the executive and judiciary on their toes and scratches at the professional honor of many officials. Funke's fatigue with life leads him to believe that he no longer must abide by any rules. In his eyes, it doesn't matter anyway. And so, he plans his first crime.

After the successful extortion of the KaDeWe in 1988, a loot of 500 000 DM and after Arno has exchanged the registered bills of his loot abroad, he is now a made man. The constant and crippling money worries are a thing of the past. He has also sworn off alcohol. But despite everything, the depressive cannot feel the relief he had hoped for and the feelings of happiness he had longed for. No matter what he does with his wealth, he feels no joy. Together with a friend, the car sprayer treats himself to a debauched vacation in the Philippines. He stays there for six months, meets a local woman, and falls head over heels in love with her. After the newly in love couple gets married, they move into a small two-room apartment in

Berlin together. Funke hopes that he has finally found happiness. In the background, however, depressive thoughts continue to waft. Mrs. Funke has no idea where her newlywed husband really gets the money with which he pays the rent and the incidental costs of daily life. She does not know that he does not finance the family exclusively with his self-employment.

Marital bliss is crowned when Arno's wife gives birth to their son. But in the meantime, the proud father is again plagued by existential fears. Most of the half million DM has already been used up. In the meantime, Arno has also consulted a doctor about his mental health. The doctor determined that the cause of Funke's depression was years of inhaling toxic solvents. It will take a long time for his body to recover from that. Arno then decided to stop living off his wages as a car sprayer so as not to put his mental health at further risk. The logical consequence of this decision was to initially continue to live off the money captured from the extortion of the KaDeWe. But it was also logical that without work no further money would follow. Funke still has DM 100,000 (about 55.000 USD) on the high side, hidden under the sink in the kitchen of his rented apartment, when fear for the financial future of his small family overtakes him. But the father knows how to help himself in a tried and tested way.

Every morning, Funke sets off for his workshop; pretends to his wife that he has a regular working day. But instead of painting cars and motorcycles, Arno uses his technical ingenuity to construct a bomb. Satisfied with his construction, he carefully packs it into his car and sets off for northern Germany.

On the night of June 13, 1992, the pipe bomb detonates in the china department of a Karstadt store in Hamburg. Almost all the goods are destroyed by the force of the explosion; the material damage caused is considerable. The management received a blackmail letter. They are to pay one million DM if they do not want to risk further disasters. To signal their willingness to pay, the blackmailer asks them to place an ad in Hamburg's evening paper with the sentence: "Dagobert sends his regards to his nephews." Hamburg police officers believe they see parallels to the KaDeWe extortion in 1988. Is Dagobert, as the blackmailer calls himself in reference to the famous comic duck Dagobert Duck (in English: Scrooge McDuck), a serial offender? If they are correct in their assumption, then a money transfer from a moving train is to be assumed. And indeed, the investigators were proved right. Two weeks later, the officers receive a phone call. Dagobert, the blackmailer, answers at the other end of the line. He directs the police officers to a station locker. Here they find further instructions and an ingenious drop device with a time switch. They are to stow the required one million DM in this construct and attach it to the last car of the “Käthe Kollwitz” intercity train.

On August 14, 1992, the train left Hamburg at 4:40 p.m. and headed for Berlin. The police had little time to take a close look at and analyze the technology of the dropping device, which could be attached to the train part by means of suction cups. Nevertheless, they managed to read the timer. After calculating the drop time, they were able to locate the place, about 100 km beyond Hamburg, where Dagobert would have to be to receive the extortion money. Several police officers positioned themselves inconspicuously along the railroad line to apprehend the blackmailer.

But it is not that simple. Funke fooled the officers. The timer was a simple trick to mislead the police. Using a remote control, Arno triggers the drop device shortly after the Intercity has passed the Hamburg city border. It takes time for the surprised police officers, who are in the last car of the train, to stop the train to give chase. Dagobert is already long gone by then. But the cunning blackmailer quickly loses his winning smile when he opens the money package. On the outside are four 1000 DM bills (about 2500 USD), but inside the package is filled only with scraps of paper and old batteries.

A risky, but understandable action by the Hamburg police. They know that they are dealing with a serial offender who was also active in 1988. If they now send him extorted cash again, they can be sure that the perpetrator will appear on the scene again in the foreseeable future. This must be prevented. Even if this means they could put Dagobert in a tight spot. And that is exactly what happens.

Funke feels that he is not being taken seriously by the officials. He knows that he now must "do one up" to lend weight to his demand. Dagobert makes a highly explosive firebomb filled with nuts and bolts. It is the night of September 9, 1992, when he detonates it in a Karstadt store in Bremen. The explosion triggers a fire. Goods that are not damaged by the force of the detonation fall victim to the flames. If the goods are not in the path of the fire, they are ruined by the incipient sprinkler system. That night, Funke causes property damage of 6 million DM (about 3 million USD). No one knows how far the bomber will go; whether he would also kill to get his money claim? Even experts who are trying to create a perpetrator profile on Dagobert are at odds about this.

Barely 2 months later; it is October 29, 1992, the bomber again demands a money package from the Karstadt chain. The blackmailer sets off on a bicycle to a railroad track in the Charlottenburg district of Berlin. Here he wants to give the signal to the money messenger in the last train carriage to throw the money package out of the train. But Dagobert has become more careless.

For example, while preparing for the handover, he does not scout out an escape route. As he pedals his bicycle through Charlottenburg, he is already being shadowed by plainclothes officers without even suspecting anything. All of Berlin's police officers are itching to finally get Dagobert under lock and key, so they are extra vigilant and alert. A circumstance that could be the undoing of the blackmailer Arno Funke. However, the fact that the policemen discover the little man cycling along the railroad line in the dark is pure coincidence.

The man gets off his bicycle and leans it against a tree. A few meters of walking, then he is standing by the railroad tracks. A bush gives him a bit of cover. Soon he sees the lights of the approaching train; feels the vibrations under his feet. "First car, second car, third car," Funke counts along in a whisper, "second to last car .... Now!" At the same moment, he presses a button that triggers a signal telling the money messenger to now throw the package out the train window. The package comes flying too, but at the same time Funke notices a multitude of frantically talking men from the train compartment. "Crap!" he curses. Now Dagobert also realizes that he has put himself in a position where his arrest could be imminent. Arno has no more head for the money package lying on the ground. With a heavy heart, he leaves the bundle on the floor. No great loss. It's another box filled only with scraps of paper and old batteries. However, the blackmailer cannot know that at this point.

He turns around and runs. "Just get out of here! Quick to the bike and then off!" it races through his head. At the same moment, a police officer rushes toward him. "Sometimes, only a few leaves lie between hero and loser," the officer summarizes later. For as he sprints toward Dagobert, he slips and falls onto the forest floor. Valuable seconds that allow the blackmailer to jump on his bike and speed off. He heads straight for the colleague of the policeman lying on the ground. In a daring evasive maneuver, however, Arno manages to escape even this officer, despite the very narrow roadway. Some time passes before the policemen can start pursuing Dagobert in their car. But they lose sight of him. And as if all this were not humiliation enough, the failed arrest is also reported long and wide in the press. Except that the journalists replace the wet leaves that brought the policeman down with a dog turd, thus severely counting Dagobert's hunters down. The next day, Germany's best-known tabloid headlines, "Bad luck for police: slip on dog poop brought Karstadt blackmailer "Dagobert" freedom." There is now talk of the "dog poop aria." The nerves of all police officers involved are on edge; frustration is spreading. Especially because the population actually sympathizes with the blackmailer, who always manages to outsmart the police officers, and seems to think the officers are complete idiots. For the investigators, this is incomprehensible. In a telephone survey by a TV station asking the question "Do you have secret sympathy for Dagobert?", 61.3% of the respondents answered "Yes".

Arno Funke likes the fact that the public sees him as "Robin Hood" and not as a "rotten little rat". It comforts the blackmailer a little about the fact that he still hasn't captured any money. What is evident is that he will have to change his tactics the next time the money is handed over. After all, he had escaped arrest by a hair's breadth. If he were to stick to his modus operandi, the police would always have the opportunity to adjust to the familiar procedure. And Dagobert doesn't want to make it that easy for his hunters.

It is April 19, 1993, when Dagobert lets the police know that he is now ready to receive some more money. In a station locker, the blackmailer leaves the officers a key and further instructions. They are to make their way to a parking lot in southern Berlin. There they would find a grit box secured with a lock to which the key from the locker would fit. The emergency services are very surprised. In the meantime, there have already been ten failed money transfers and a train always played the central role. Of course, all the concepts worked out and the further action of the police were based on this circumstance. And now this. The officers get into their car and set off for the specified location near Berlin's Britz-Süd subway station.

Once there, they discover the announced litter sand box, secured with a lock, at the edge of the parking lot. The police officers take a close look at it. From the outside they can see nothing unusual. "What's under the box?" asks one of the officers. His colleague tries to lift the chest. In vain. "Forget it, it's so heavy, I can't move it a millimeter," he gasps. The other investigator puts the key in the lock. It fits. Carefully, they lift the lid and immediately discover the reason why the chest can't be moved. It is filled almost to the brim with granules. On top is a note. "Put the money inside and close the lid," the men read. They rummage through the granules, but there doesn't seem to be anything else in the box. So, they put the money package in the chest and close the lid. Now they must wait…hour after hour. Of course, some of the plainclothesmen in their cover wonder if Dagobert really thinks they'll let the grit box with the money packet out of their sight for even a moment. As soon as Dagobert opens the chest, they would seize it and the Punch and Judy show would finally come to an end.

Two officers are sitting in their car, watching the area around the box, when an alarm suddenly sounds. The two look at each other questioningly. The alarm indicates that the money package has been moved. They had specially hidden a motion detector in the package so that they would not miss it in the dark of night when the extortionist took his loot. "Must be a technical error," speculates one of the men. Because they have a good view of the chest, and everything seems quiet, no one approaches the box. Thus, the waiting continues. After another hour, one of the policemen decides to sneak up to the grit box and carefully peek inside. Then the shock: the chest is empty! The psychological pressure on the task force and their superiors increases immeasurably. How would Dagobert react if he once again found only scraps of paper instead of money? Will he carry out his threat and set off another bomb? Are lives at risk now? In any case, the police officers are sure to be scorned and ridiculed by the public and the press.

Once again, Arno Funke has tricked the officers. He had placed the grit box on a manhole to a storm drain, the cover of which he removed. He covered the manhole with a thin layer of concrete. He hid a radio microphone in the chest filled with granules. This allowed him to listen in on what the officers were discussing on the surface and when he could strike without danger. When Funke heard the officers moving away from the chest, he crept through the underground tunnel to his self-concreted lid. Using a screwdriver, he crumbled the concrete. There was already a square opening in the bottom of the chest, large enough to pull his prey through. When the granules had trickled down, he got hold of the money package. That was the moment the motion detector went off, which the officers mistakenly judged to be a technical false alarm. Immediately, Funke opened the package. Dagobert's frustration could hardly be put into words when he saw the contents.

The Berlin police now not only have to contend with their adversary and the vilification by the press - the rumor is also growing that Dagobert could come from within the ranks of the Berlin police. Why else would the blackmailer keep escaping? Distrust among the officers grows, and in the operational planning they weigh up who is allowed to receive what information. A circumstance that further complicates the work of the police and unsettles the officers. But the rumor cannot be substantiated. The only thing that is certain is that the classic method of arresting the blackmailer when he hands over the money has failed in the Dagobert case. The police must change their strategy.

And it plays into their hands that the blackmailer also changes his approach. Instead of using a computer to play messages over the phone, Dagobert now calls the Berlin officers himself from public phone booths. The experts interpret his behavior as meaning that he, too, is now slowly but surely losing patience and is no longer willing to invest so much time in preparing the umpteenth handover of money, only to receive scraps of paper again. This new circumstance is now the basis for the renewed strategy of the emergency services: they want to catch the blackmailer when he calls from a phone booth to announce a new handover of money.

This is an enormous effort for the Berlin police, because it means that all phone booths must be monitored. But it is no use because they finally need a success. Meanwhile, one or the other officer even feels personally attacked by Dagobert's actions. Not a nice feeling, but it increases the ambition and the determination of the police officers. 3,000 plainclothes officers are rounded up and put on surveillance of dozens of phone booths. For June 30, 1993, Dagobert has announced another call to the officers with instructions. Since the blackmailer has so far always called from the western part of the city, the police post two civilian task forces at each of the 1,500 public phone booths in western Berlin; ready to finally catch the perpetrator. However, the Berlin police's operational concept collapses within a few seconds when Dagobert actually calls them - but the officers realize that Dagobert is in a phone booth in the eastern part of the city. Another bitter setback for the hunters.

But Funke's disappointment also continues to grow. He feels that he is not being taken seriously and feels compelled to increase the pressure on the police. They should finally understand how serious he is,so the blackmailer builds another explosive device. This time, however, he goes one step further: While he has been able to minimize the risk of injuring or even killing other people in his bombings by carrying out his attacks exclusively at night up to now, he now takes no account of losses.

On December 6, 1993, in the middle of the Christmas shopping season, Funke detonates his homemade explosive device in the elevator of a Karstadt store in Berlin. During opening hours. It is very fortunate that no one is injured. Dagobert is also relieved. He has shown the Berlin police what he is capable of, but he has not physically harmed anyone. And he achieves what he wanted: the Karstadt company, but also the police, begin to doubt their previous strategy. Apparently, the blackmailer is really willing to accept hurting innocent people or even taking their lives. This assessment is reinforced by a letter from Dagobert, which he sends after the bombing: "...Apparently, the police psychologist believes that I am not capable of killing people. I will prove you wrong!"

Things are getting too hot for Karstadt's management. They urge the investigators to put real cash in the money package at the next money transfer to finally put an end to the spook.

Then the time has come, on January 22, 1994, the next money handover is imminent. Dagobert directs the money messenger to an abandoned railroad yard. On the tracks, the investigators find a technical masterpiece: a mini lorry designed and built by Dagobert himself. In the larger variation, a lorry is a rail transport wagon with a tipping trough for removing sand or rubble, for example. As instructed, the official places the money package containing the required DM 1.4 million (about 718 000 USD) on the small construction and presses a button. The lorry then starts chugging away but picks up speed so quickly that the officers hardly have a chance to follow it through the rough terrain. Not that they didn't try. But the shrewd blackmailer has of course reckoned with this and set up several trip wires as a precaution. The running policemen fall and set off a lot of pyrotechnics by touching the wires. And so 1.4 million DM disappears into the night.

Dagobert, who is waiting in his hiding place at the edge of the railroad tracks for the arrival of his self-made gliding sled, is startled by the deafeningly loud explosions of the firecrackers. The light of several flashlights blinds him. Funke jumps out of his hiding place in panic, flees without waiting for the mini-lore, and escapes his pursuers.

The next day, Arno reads in the newspaper that he came closer than ever to his extortion money yesterday: just 23 meters from his hiding place by the railroad tracks, the mini lorry jumped out of the rails. That's no consolation, however, because Funke desperately needs money. The loot from the KaDeWe extortion has now been completely used up. He and his small family now live on state welfare. The family man has borrowed money for the elaborate and costly preparations for the fruitless money transfers. He is at the same point as six years ago, before his first extortion:

penniless and in debt. But he does not want to take the last step and become a murderer as much as he would like to have this 1.4 million DM. So, the blackmailer hatches a new plan.

On April 20, 1994, Dagobert telephones the police again and requests another money delivery. The investigators succeed in locating the public phone booth. A two-man mobile task force is immediately dispatched. On their way to the scene, the officers notice a white compact car. A folding bicycle is stowed in the back seat. The driver is sitting at the wheel with his shoulders slumped, his elbows on the edge of the window, his chin propped up with one hand. His facial expression seems heavy with thought. One of the officers has the license plate of the small car checked via the control center. It is a rental car. From the car rental agency, the police officers learn that the driver rented the car at a time that corresponded with a phone call from Dagobert and that the rental contract was extended by the customer on the day of a failed money transfer. This cannot be a coincidence! The Berlin police receive the name and full address of the customer from the car rental company. From now on, Arno Funke is under surveillance.

It is April 22, 1994, when the observing officers watch Funke leave his apartment building with a little boy. He puts the boy into the rental car and drives off.

The investigators follow him. Their route leads them to a daycare center. The father takes the child to the facility, gets back into his car, and drives off. The officers are close behind him. Everything seems so bourgeois and normal to the two police officers that they slowly begin to doubt whether they are really following Dagobert, the department store extortionist. Nevertheless, it is the hottest lead since the beginning of this crime series. They can't let their guard down now.

10:15, a Karstadt store in Berlin: the phone in the management's office rings. On the other end of the line: Dagobert. Another attempt to relieve the department store chain of DM 1.4 million. When the blackmailer ends the phone call, he steps out of the phone booth onto the street. Suddenly, a dark BMW shoots around the corner with screeching tires. Before Funke can react, the two officers rush out of their car toward him and handcuff him. "I'm Dagobert," the arrested man says to them in no uncertain terms. It's done - after six long years of hunting, the cat has caught the mouse.

In the summer of 1996, the trial of the department store extortionist takes place. Funke is sentenced in the second instance to nine years in prison for predatory extortion and to pay DM 2.5 million (around 1.2 million USD) in damages to Karstadt. The brain-organic disorder, triggered by the solvent vapors, is credited to the defendant as a reduction of guilt. His wife, who had no idea of her husband's criminal double life, divorces him. After six years of imprisonment in Plötzensee Prison, Arno Funke is released in August 2000 for good behavior. At the time of his release, his son is 10 years old. Now, in freedom, he meets his boy regularly.

During his imprisonment, the blackmailer begins to pass his time by drawing caricatures. His works came to the attention of the humor and satire magazine "Eulenspiegel," for which Funke still works as a cartoonist. He also created caricature posters for the election campaign of the Left Party. In the beginning, he drew by hand, but today he creates his caricatures on the computer. But it is not only drawing that suits the former prisoner. In 1998, he published his autobiography "My Life as Dagobert," followed by "Ente kross," a book of caricatures and related stories.

Funke uses his popularity with the public to earn his salary and become debt-free. Among other things, he gives lectures to students about resocialization; appears on theater stages with his own program "Erbrechen lohnt sich nicht" ("Vomiting is not worth it"), in true Funke fashion. Even after decades, the blackmailer who fooled the police is still a topic of conversation and a popular guest on entertainment shows. "Some people think that when I appear, there must be the smell of sulfur in the air," the former inmate joked in an interview with the Rheinische Post. You could say he's a C-list celebrity. It's no surprise that he flickered across Germany's screens in 2013 as a candidate in the jungle camp on RTL. If he's not crowned jungle king, he collects a hefty fee of 40,000 euros, which he passes on directly to Karstadt.

Funke, who is now 71 years old, has never been convicted of a crime. He has paid the damages to Karstadt in full and is now debt-free. He is a resocialized citizen. His path back into society, back into a life without crime, is considered exemplary. The old man rarely thinks back to his crimes. " That is far away," he says. Does he regret his actions? He has his problems with the word remorse, Dagobert tells the Rheinische Post in an interview. In prison, he says, he has met many inmates who speak of remorse but feel sorry for themselves. He himself can only say: he would never do anything like the department store extortions as Dagobert again.

Evil will always pile up with evils
And, if it cannot kill you, only torment you more and more and more with each day torment you.

- Johann Wolfgang von Goethe (1749 - 1832),
German poet -

CHAPTER 5

Farmer seeks wife

When Berlin-born Sigrid K. does housework, she often turns on the TV to have a little company while she does so. Depending on the time of day, the pensioner with the chin-length, silver hair and thin lips then amuses herself with quirky trash shows, exciting documentaries or gives vent to her indignation at news from around the world. But the news that flickers across the screen on the afternoon of April 29, 2016, makes Sigrid K. prick up her ears.

The 75-year-old is ironing when a report on the TV program "Brisant," produced by MDR (Mitteldeutscher Rundfunk), tells of a woman who was hospitalized a few days earlier with serious injuries. The woman had been so badly abused by her partner and his sister on a farm in Bosseborn that she succumbed to her injuries in hospital. Meanwhile, a preliminary investigation has been initiated against the alleged perpetrators; the two are in custody.

When Sigrid K. sees the pictures of the farmhouse and a reporter names the address, Saatweg number 6, her blood instantly freezes in her veins. Doesn't her daughter Anika live in this house, together with her husband Wilfried and his sister Angelika?

The pensioner unplugs the iron and rushes to the phone. Desperately, she bombards her daughter with messages and calls, but can't reach her. She feels uneasy. Two weeks earlier, she had been in contact with Anika. She wrote that everything was fine and that she was doing well. But now? Is it possible that ...? No! Sigrid cannot and does not want to think about that. Anika is surely being questioned by the police as a witness and will report back soon. And indeed: a few minutes later the phone rings.

"Hello?!?"

Through the receiver, however, it is not her daughter's voice that reaches her, but that of her partner: "Sigrid, you must urgently turn on the television! They're reporting on the news about ..."

"I know," Sigrid K. interrupts him, "that house in Höxter-Bosseborn ... we were there, weren't we? Isn't that where Anika lives?"

Her partner advises her to ask the police about her daughter's condition, which Sigrid K. does immediately. She hangs up and dials the number of a police officer friend. He promises to check on Anika's condition with his colleagues in Höxter and to get back to her as soon as possible.

When Sigrid K.'s phone rings again, it is frighteningly quiet at the other end of the line. "I'm sorry ... Sigrid ... but ... Anika is no longer alive."

At these words, the 75-year-old's heart drops; her emotions ride a roller coaster. Her daughter: dead? That can't be! "Are you sure about that?"

Silence again. "Yes," the policeman then says. "I think it's better if you come to Höxter with your partner. The colleagues will then explain everything to you in peace."

Sigrid thanks her friend for the information, hangs up and dials her partner's number with trembling hands. She tells him what is supposed to have happened, and the two agree to drive to Höxter that same evening. They hope that all this is just a terrible mistake.

"Mrs. K., I would like to express my sincere sympathy and deep condolences to you." It is shortly before noon. Anika's mother and her partner are sitting across from a policewoman in a Höxter police office and are confronted with the bitter truth: Anika is dead.

"It can't be!" cries Sigrid, bursting into tears. Her partner grabs her by the shoulders and talks to her soothingly. He wants to know from the policewoman if Anika is the woman reported in the news. "No," the officer replies.

This woman had also lived on the farm; to all intents and purposes, she was Anika's successor. It is assumed that terrible things happened in this house, she said.

"Two weeks ago, I was still writing to Anika," Sigrid sobs, "she said she was fine and I needn't worry." The policewoman tears her eyes open. "Impossible," she says, "your daughter has been dead for almost two years."

Anika E. was born in 1980, the third of three girls, in Dinkelhausen, a district of the small town of Uslar in Lower Saxony. She is a latecomer; her two sisters are already of age when she is born. Despite the age difference, the siblings have a close relationship, and the animal-loving Anika also has a very intimate relationship with her mother - the two never miss an opportunity to share this with each other.

Anika enjoys her life. Photos in her parents' house show the young girl with the blue eyes, the roundish face, the pointed nose, and the narrow lips playing in the garden, together with her siblings or with animals in her arms. In addition, Anika often dares to make optical changes, such as her hairstyle, whose color and length she changes according to her mood.

Although she is diagnosed with a developmental disorder and initially attends a special school, Anika leaves school with a successful degree, obtains a driver's license and begins an apprenticeship as a housekeeper, which she also completes successfully. Afterwards, she works in a nursing home for the elderly, where she is valued above all for the loving, good-natured and obliging way in which she cares for the seniors.

There's only one thing that doesn't quite work out: love. Anika, who is now 33, simply can't find the right man for life - until she comes across a personal ad in the newspaper in the summer of 2013 with the headline " Farmer Seeks Wife." According to the ad, a certain Wilfried from Höxter-Bosseborn, 45 years old, 1.88 m tall, 108 kg, is looking for a nice partner for life. He describes himself as romantic, nature-loving, sweet, and nice. Since the ad appeals to her, Anika enters the number that Wilfried has attached to his ad into her phone and goes to see the farmer.

The chemistry between the two is harmonic right away and they keep in regular contact from now on. Wilfried texts his sweetheart from morning to night, sends her photos and voice messages, and tells her about himself and his daily life on the farm. According to the text, he, a sturdy man with a thick, knobby nose, deep receding hairline and big ears, lives together with his sister Angelika in a beautiful little house and looks after the geese, pigs, and chickens there.

Anika's cell phone jingles and vibrates all the time; she constantly walks around the house with her eyes downcast. When the whole thing gets to the point that Anika leaps up, head over heels, and disappears into her room even while they are eating together, when a message from her sweetheart appears on the display, her mother gets angry: "Can't you just once, just while we're sitting here together, push your Wilfried aside for a moment?"

"Leave me be!" retorts Anika. She can't understand her mother's anger. Why isn't she just happy that her daughter has finally found the right man for her life?

After a few weeks of intensive digital contact, Wilfried makes it unmistakably clear to the 33-year-old that there would only be a future for him if she were to marry him as soon as possible. Anika should move in with him so that they could start a family together and settle down - otherwise the relationship would make no sense to him.

Anika immediately agrees. The 33-year-old is not bothered by the fact that Wilfried's sister Angelika lives in the house with him. After all, she knows that almost all farms are family-run.

But when the geriatric nurse sees her new home for the first time, her dream of a fairytale life bursts like a soap bubble. The pretty little house that Wilfried had always described to her doesn't exist. Instead, Anika is standing in front of the wooden entrance door of a run-down hovel - a two-story single-family house with gray facades, a red tile roof and an attached barn. Piles of garbage pile up to the ceiling in every room, the wet walls are infested with mold, the wallpaper in the kitchen is run down.

Although Anika has a queasy feeling, she makes up her mind and pushes her doubts aside. All she wants are happy years together with the love of her life. Who cares about the surroundings?

When Anika steps over the threshold, however, the horror really begins for her. Her future husband's initial affectionate manner is abruptly over. He forces her to hand over all her personal belongings, such as her cell phone and her wallet, along with their contents. The 33-year-old is also forbidden to have any contact with her neighbors or the outside world; she is only allowed to send her mother messages now and then and to talk to her on the phone under strict supervision.

In the following weeks, Wilfried treats his girlfriend like a slave. Anika must quit her job as a geriatric nurse to serve him as a housewife. She cleans, cooks, and brings him tea at set times. When he talks to her, she must look him in the eye and not contradict him. If she does not follow the rules, she is punished. With every day Anika spends in the house, she forfeits a bit more of her freedom. It is not long before the first smack lands in the face of the trained housekeeper. However, she is so blinded by her love for Wilfried that she does not defend herself and overlooks all this. She thinks that Wilfried's behavior towards her must be justified.

On the morning of October 18, 2013, the time has come: Wilfried and Anika say "I do" at the registry office in Höxter. The bride is dressed in a black blouse, the groom wears a dark gray suit with a white shirt and red and black striped tie, and both have an orange paper butterfly on their lapels.

Since the marriage, at Wilfried's will, takes place behind closed doors, Sister Angelika is the only one allowed to attend the ceremony as a guest. Not even Anika's mother, who has no idea of the upcoming wedding anyway, is allowed to stand by her daughter on this great day. After the wedding ceremony, sister Angelika, as the new sister-in-law, takes a souvenir photo, and then the three of them go out for breakfast.

Sigrid K. only finds out by chance that her daughter has married. In November 2013, she unsuccessfully tries to reach Anika by phone to inquire about her health. When the answering machine comes on, the 33-year-old's voice answers with a new last name: "Anika W."

"Oh, are you married now?" speaks Sigrid on the voicemail. "Too bad we weren't there."

When Anika checks in later, she apologizes to her mother. Wilfried had not wanted her family to know about the wedding. Even though Sigrid K. accepts this circumstance, she does not want to accept her daughter's marriage without comment and drives to Höxter-

Bosseborn with her partner to give the newlyweds a little money. The 73-year-old pensioner hopes to finally meet her son-in-law in person on this occasion.

However, this idea vanishes into thin air, because when Sigrid and her partner arrive at Saatweg 6, the front door remains closed even after ringing the bell several times. They have no choice but to put the envelope in the mailbox and leave.

Shortly before Christmas 2013, Anika once again returns to her hometown of Uslar to pay her mother a visit. Although it is the first time in almost half a year that the two can embrace each other again, an uncomfortable distance has crept between them. Sigrid explains to her daughter that although she thinks it is nice that she is now married and seems to have found the man of her dreams, she is still a little disappointed that Anika continues to cut herself off from her family. Anika takes note of this comment with a tired smile. All the while, she seems nervous and on the go; not half an hour after her arrival, she already wants to leave.

When saying goodbye, Sigrid offers her daughter to pack a few belongings left behind and take them with her, but Anika refuses. When asked if Anika was there by car, the 33-year-old explains that her sister-in-law Angelika drove her here and is waiting for her in front of the house. "Oh, that's nice," Sigrid says. "Shall I walk you to the car?

Then I can meet her." "I'd rather not," Anika counters, "you don't want to meet her." What Anika means by this; her mother cannot yet guess.

Angelica is a small woman, with a fringed Prince Valiant hairdo, deep blue eyes, crooked nose, and a wart below her narrow mouth from which rotten teeth protrude. In the coming weeks, it is she who gradually transforms Wilfried's mostly psychological torture of his wife into physical violence.

Anika is beaten and abused more and more often by Angelika and Wilfried. Tufts of her hair are pulled out, her skin is scalded with boiling hot water, she is pushed down the stairs or tortured with a stun gun. She usually endures all this when Wilfried and Angelika are in a mood or when they accuse Anika of misconduct. All the tasks imposed on her are designed in such a way that sooner or later Wilfried's bride-to-be fails to carry them out and is horribly punished by her tormentors.

The trained housekeeper becomes increasingly emaciated because she only occasionally gets something to eat. And when she does, the strictly rationed food is so heavily spiced that Anika suffers from a terrible feeling of thirst after eating it. The most she gets to drink, however, is Wilfried's urine.

At night, she is handcuffed to a radiator naked or forced to sleep in the bathtub; she is not allowed to use the toilet. Wilfried and Angelika often arrange for Anika to wet herself during the night to have a reason to punish her in the morning.

On August 3, 2014, Anika succumbs to her severe injuries. In the last days of her life, she can hardly speak, complains of dizziness, and seems unable to perceive anything. Wilfried and Angelika then lock her up in the barn overnight. The next morning, they notice that their victim's condition has deteriorated dramatically. But instead of immediately calling an ambulance, they leave the barn door open to see if Anika attempts to escape. She initially drags herself a few steps towards freedom, but then collapses and hits her head on the ground. With her last strength, she crawls back to her sleeping place, collapses again, and does not move again; the next day she is dead.

Wilfried wants to bury Anika's body under the manure pile or throw it into the cesspool, but Angelika persuades him to put her victim's emaciated and battered body in the freezer for the time being.

They close Anika's eyes and place her in the white box with a hinged lid. However, since Anika's body doesn't quite fit inside, Angelika pushes her head down far and places a pizza on top. Then they flip the lid of the chest shut.

A few days later, the brother and sister drive to a hardware store and buy a saw and latex gloves. It is too risky for them to keep Anika's mortal remains in the house - the corpse is to be cut up.

From now on, Angelica cuts off pieces of Anika every night, chops them up and burns them in the oven. In order not to alarm the neighbors with the noise of the saw, Angelika puts a CD player next to the freezer and listens to loud music. Wilfried, meanwhile, sleeps in the living room and leaves all the hard work to his sister.

When the corpse is completely dismembered and burned, Wilfried and Angelika dispose of the stove and the freezer and add the ashes to a bag of grit. They then drive off in their car to scatter the mixture on the road. Then Wilfried's last wife is just a memory.

To cover up Anika's disappearance, the two claim that Anika has moved to Amsterdam. In addition, Angelika continues to send messages to her mother in Anika's name. "Anika" affirms that she is fine and that her mother has nothing to worry about. She does not want to make any phone calls and does not receive any visitors. Sigrid K. has no idea of her daughter's fate and accepts "her" will. For 635 days.

April 21, 2016. It is shortly after 10 pm. 41-year-old Susanne F. lies huddled in the back seat of the white Opel Corsa Combo. Her emaciated body is covered with hematomas, her muscles cramp again and again. Under

Susanne are two spread-out garbage bags to prevent her from soiling the seat covers with her urine.

Peering through her half-closed eyelids, Susanne can make out the outlines of two figures on the front seats. They are the people who abused and tortured her for months: Wilfried and Angelika. Every now and then, their faces are illuminated for a brief moment by the yellow light of the streetlamps. The two have decided to take their victim back to Bad Gandersheim, a spa town in the Northeim district of Lower Saxony, to die.

Susanne keeps dozing off on the hellish drive, when the car suddenly stalls and starts making strange noises. "You've got to be kidding me," Angelika curses and vigorously stomps the gas pedal several times, "come on!" The car slows down, however, until it finally comes to a stop at a bus stop on Bundestraße 64 in Eschershausen.

Angelika gets out of the Corsa and hurries to one of the nearby apartment buildings. She rings the bell and asks the resident to use the phone; she had broken down with the car and wanted to call a cab.

When she returns to Wilfried, he points to Susanne with a worried look: "Look, she's cramping like crazy."

Angelica grimaces. At the same moment, she sees the lights of two large headlights coming at her from a distance. It's the cab she ordered, stopping next to the

Corsa Combo. The clock hands point to five minutes past half past ten.

"Did you order a cab?" the driver wants to know. "Yes," Angelika calls out, taking another look at Susanne, "but actually we need an emergency ambulance!"

The cab driver is visibly taken aback, but hands Wilfried and Angelika his business card anyway before driving off again.

At 10:53 p.m., the Northeim control center receives an emergency call. Angelika answers the phone and claims that an acquaintance of hers is not feeling well and therefore urgently needs an emergency doctor. She gives the street and the approximate location, then hangs up.

Minutes later, the cold, clear night air is filled with the sound of a siren and the ambulance's signal light bathes the surroundings in a rich blue.

The paramedics immediately notice that Susanne is dressed far too thinly, despite the almost wintry temperatures. They detect severe hypothermia. In addition, the man and woman with whom the patient is traveling seem extremely strange to them. Angelica, who at first does not want to reveal her name to the helpers, claims that Susanne F. has no relatives and lives in a women's shelter in Gelsenkirchen.

Since the injuries of the meanwhile unresponsive woman are too serious, she is immediately put into the ambulance and taken to the Helios Hospital in Northeim; in the meantime, Wilfried and Angelika let themselves be brought back to Höxter-Bosseborn by the cab driver who was called in again. Did they possibly get off lightly after all?

One hour later, Susanne F. succumbs to her injuries. The doctors find several marks on her body, bruises, scabbed wounds, cuts and several puncture marks on her arms and legs. Almost nothing is left of her once blond, plump hair; even some toenails have already come off.

That same night, the Helios Hospital informs the police in Göttingen, some 25 kilometers away, of an "unexplained death" - the start of the investigation into what is probably one of the most spectacular and at the same time cruelest German crimes of the 21st century.

After the autopsy of the body reveals a homicide by blunt force trauma to the victim's skull and torso, the police of North Rhine-Westphalia, together with the Bielefeld homicide unit, establish the 40-member "Bosseborn" homicide unit, which arrests Wilfried and Angelika W. as the suspected perpetrators on April 27, 2016, five days after Susanne's death. One day later, the Höxter District Court issues an arrest warrant against both for manslaughter. From now on, the farm at Saatweg 6 is officially designated as the scene of the crime and the doors are sealed.

During a first search of the house, the forensics team digs out numerous documents, photographs, and video recordings of several women from several meters of garbage, which give the investigators reason to believe that Susanne is not the only one who fell victim to Wilfried's and Angelica's machinations - and they are to be proven right.

A few days later, a 51-year-old woman named Christel P. from the Berlin area comes forward, claiming that she too was held captive in the "Höxter House of Horrors," as the media now impressively headline it, and that she was abused by Wilfried and Angelika W. The police then follow up on this lead.

When the police pursue this lead and send a team of investigators from Bielefeld to Berlin for questioning, the officers come face to face with a woman with chin-length hair, dark eyes and a face marked by life, who reveals shocking details of her time at Saatweg number 6, between late 2011 and early 2012.

Christel P. reports that she also got in touch with Wilfried through an ad in the newspaper. They got along well and after a few phone calls Wilfried offered to pick her up from her home by car and take her to Höxter. However, since he did not have a driver's license, his sister

Angelika, who lived with him in his house, would come along.

When the brother and sister came one cold afternoon in December 2011 in a kind of "white dog catcher car", Christel P. was already standing expectantly and with packed bags in front of her former home. For her, her newfound love was a step into a new life, because since her divorce from her husband two years earlier, the trained concrete worker had kept her head above water with odd jobs and lived alone in a gray prefabricated building in Magdeburg.

After a hasty announcement and a short chat, it was decided by mutual agreement to postpone the welcoming ceremony to a later time because of the upcoming almost two-and-a-half-hour drive back to Höxter-Bosseborn.

On the way to the car, Wilfried and Angelika were anything but obliging, Since there was allegedly no more room in the front part of the car, Christel was instructed to take a seat in the loading area, cut off from her chauffeurs by a separating grid.

When the trio arrived late at night in Höxter-Bosseborn, Wilfried had shown his new girlfriend the geese, pigs, and chickens before they all went to sleep in the living room, the only heated room in the house; Wilfried and Christel on the couch, Angelika on a mattress next to it.

Within the first three weeks, the new beginning Christel had hoped for seemed to have succeeded: Wilfried showed himself from his best side, was affectionate and warm. For the then 47-year-old there is no longer any doubt - she has finally found the man for her life. When asked by the officials whether she could really have imagined living on the run-down farm forever, Christel confesses that she thought something could be done with the house. But such renovations also cost a lot of money, the officials note. Money that the W. family obviously didn't have. Didn't that make Christel wonder?

"I didn't ask any questions," she says.

At the beginning of January 2012, the mood suddenly changed. Christel is just sitting on the sofa, when Wilfried hits his girlfriend "out of the blue" with full force right in the face.

"I was totally flabbergasted, after all I didn't know what I was supposed to have done," the woman explains to the police officers. "I then went to a corner and cried."

From then on, she says, the farmer's affectionate and cordial manner came to an end. He regularly beat her black and blue with his fist right in the stomach. Christel felt trapped and begged her boyfriend several times to let her go back home.

"Go on!" Wilfried had grumbled at her, but escape seemed impossible through the steadily locked doors and windows.

"I wasn't alone for a second," Christel reports, "they took everything from me: my cell phone, my wallet with all my papers, the key to my apartment in Magdeburg ... simply everything. I couldn't just walk out and leave."

When she once tried to alert the neighbors to her situation, she says, she was horribly punished for it.

"Wilfried threw me to the floor in the kitchen and choked me so much that I almost passed out. After that, Angelika sprayed pepper spray in my face."

The following weeks were torture for Christel P. Angelika had shorn her hair, chained her in the barn with the pigs, and forced her to stand barefoot in the manure. Since Christel was not allowed to go to the toilet at night, she had to use the cat's litter box out of necessity and under constant observation of her tormentors who watched her suffer, laughing maliciously.

After a "considerable confrontation" in spring 2012, during which Wilfried hit Christel in the face with a shovel, among other things, the brother and sister finally let their victim go. But they did not make it quite so easy for Christel P., as the 51-year-old reports. Before they put the completely exhausted woman at the station Bielefeld into a train to Magdeburg, they requested Christel to explain to the police in writing that she had gotten her wounds by falling down the stairs.

When she arrived home, Christel had moved a cupboard in front of the apartment door and did not dare to go out on the street for days. Only now, four years later, when she heard about Wilfried's and Angelica's arrest on the news, did she pluck up the courage to go to the police and tell her story.

While the apartment building at number 6 Saatweg is being cleared out at the beginning of May 2016 by officers from the North Rhine-Westphalia State Criminal Investigation Office and investigators from the "Bosseborn" homicide unit, the police receive further tips from alleged victims. In addition, the officers find numerous notes with self-incriminations in the house, signed by women held captive there. This prompts the officers to expand the investigation to a period between 1998 and 2016 - and they come across a detail that puts the case in a completely new light:

The alleged perpetrators are by no means siblings, as initially assumed by all involved - but a pair of lovers who had been married since 1999 and even gave birth to a child together; in 2013, the marriage was divorced for financial reasons.

Confronted with the new findings, Angelika claims to have once been a victim of Wilfried's violent outbursts herself. Angelika B., as she was known before marrying Wilfried, was born in Herford on January 21, 1970, and grew up on a farm in Lockhausen. As a child, she had been diagnosed with an IQ of over 120, which meant that the animal-loving Angelika was considered to have above-average talent at an early age. This was also reflected in her high sense of duty and her very good memory. Angelika reports that she always had to lend a hand on her parents' farm and never had a "best friend". After graduating from high school, she began an apprenticeship as a gardener, which she successfully completed.

After the death of her father, Angelika was urged by her mother to look for a husband, whereupon the then 29-year-old responded to the newspaper advertisement of Wilfried W. from Bochum, who was about the same age. The latter was immediately taken with Angelika and the two arranged to meet - an encounter that Angelika describes today as "love at first sight". At that first meeting, the then janitor revealed, among other things, that he was heavily in debt, which is why Angelika told him about her large savings and promised him financial support.

The wedding took place just eight weeks later; Angelika gave up her job as a gardener for the sake of her husband. The 46-year-old reports that Wilfried had already beaten and humiliated her several times by this time; among other things, he allegedly pulled a bedspread over her head and then lay on top of her. At least twenty times she had been driven to the brink of unconsciousness in this way.

In the following years, under Wilfried's instructions, she placed countless personal ads for him to lure lonely women to the house in Höxter. She herself had acted as the first contact person for the selected victims and had posed as Wilfried's sister; the women were to be kept like servants.

While Angelika admits to the deeds and presents herself as an alleged victim, her ex-husband remains silent about the accusations. Only during an interrogation, shortly after his arrest, he stated that he had not abused any of the women. According to this, his ex-wife alone was responsible for all the atrocities. But is this really true? Did Angelica act completely on her own?

The circumstantial evidence speaks against Wilfried's testimony. The reason for this is a sentence of almost three years' imprisonment from the Paderborn District Court in 1995, which the sturdy farmer received because he had kept his wife at the time in a slave-like manner and had abused her severely.

Wilfried also has a rather bumpy curriculum vitae in other respects: he was born in Bochum in 1970 and attended a special school because of his reading and spelling disability. He later moved with his mother to live with her partner on a farm in Bad Lippspringe. Initially, the young man began training as a dog handler with the British Army of the Ranks but dropped out to help on the farm. This was followed by an apprenticeship as a car mechanic.

At the age of 21, he lived on welfare and entered a relationship with a woman named Michaela; in the summer of 1994, he married another woman from Paderborn, while the relationship with Michaela continued. The latter even moved into the newlywed couple's new apartment with them and participated in the abuse of Wilfried's wife. For this crime, the couple was sentenced to prison terms of two years and nine months and one year probation, respectively.

After Wilfried was released, he met his future wife Angelika in 1999. Fourteen years after their soon-to-be marriage, the couple divorced due to financial problems, but continued to live together in their house in Höxter-Bosseborn. In October 2014, Wilfried entered what is now his third marriage with Anika, from whose mother he had also managed to obtain money to finance a kiosk at the Brakel train station.

Is Angelika really telling the truth? Was she herself a victim of her ex-husband? Did Wilfried force her into the abuse? Or did she know exactly about his past and is now using it for a theatrical story to get out of the affair?

In any case, for the Paderborn public prosecutor's office it is undisputed that both Wilfried and Angelika took part in the mistreatment of the women. Therefore, on September 21, 2016, charges of two counts of murder by omission and multiple counts of assault are brought against the defendants; the trial begins over a month later, on October 26, 2016, in the jury courtroom of the Paderborn Regional Court.

Angelika is dressed in a green anorak and hides her face behind a red briefcase from the journalists' cameras. Wilfried, on the other hand, is not afraid to show the public his round face, dotted with soft stubble. His light blue eyes, peering out from behind the lenses of black glasses, radiate complete composure and his narrow mouth has tightened into a sardonic grin.

No matter how united the two defendants may be through their long-standing marriage and their alleged common crimes - in the courtroom they are now separate people. There is a total icy atmosphere between the two; their eyes do not meet even once. As a precaution, the court has placed two court employees between them to prevent any contact.

Across from the dock sits Sigrid K., who is appearing in the trial as a joint plaintiff. It is the first time she has looked into the faces of the people who are said to have cruelly abused and killed her daughter.

After the journalists have left the hall and silence has gradually fallen, the senior prosecutor rises to read the indictment. Wilfried follows the whole thing with a calm gaze; only at the points where it says that the accused had strangled a woman does he shake his head. Angelika's eyes also rest attentively on the lips of the senior prosecutor. Only now and then does she let her gaze wander through the audience present or look up at the ceiling.

The focus of the trial for the court is the question of guilt of the two defendants. Who played which role in the "Höxter House of Horrors"? For Wilfried's and Angelika's lawyers, this question is quickly clarified: the other bears the sole blame. Neither of them wants to be able to confirm the image of their respective clients as alleged monsters. The difference lies in their intellectual capacity, says Wilfried's lawyer. While Angelica, with her "excellent memory," her IQ and her eloquence, could be considered quite manipulative, Wilfried's lawyer feared that his client's clumsy choice of words and insecure demeanor could lead to misinterpretations of his statements. For this reason, it was decided to keep Wilfried silent for the time being.

For Angelika's lawyer, on the other hand, it is undisputed that his client was manipulated by her ex-husband and driven to commit the abuse. Although she had admitted the acts, she had acted on Wilfried's sole orders.

To generate a more objective picture of the question of guilt, a forensic expert examines both defendants. She concludes that Angelika exhibits "traits of autism", uses sexuality as an "instrument of power" and cannot feel any compassion for her fellow human beings or victims. In addition, she was highly intelligent and extremely domineering and power conscious.

Wilfried, on the other hand, had the worldview of an elementary school child. He is constantly searching for "great love," but doesn't even know what that actually means. "Guilt or responsibility for the deeds cannot be taught to him," they say. He is said to be of diminished culpability.

According to the expert, the guilt is attributable to both defendants. They had developed, for them, a perfect system to trap women. However, this system was based less on the individuals, but had only worked through Wilfried's and Angelika's interaction, otherwise the abuses in Höxter would not have been possible.

On October 5, 2018, almost two years after the start of the trial and after 60 days of hearings, the Paderborn Regional Court sentenced Angelika W. to 13 years' imprisonment and her ex-husband Wilfried to 11 years' imprisonment for two counts of murder and murder by omission. For Wilfried, placement in a psychiatric clinic is additionally ordered.

With this, the court does not consider the demand of the public prosecutor's office and the joint plaintiffs, who had pleaded for a life sentence with special severity of guilt. Angelika had contributed significantly to the clarification of the crime, which ultimately had a mitigating effect on her sentence. Due to his low IQ, Wilfried is legally considered "feeble-minded" and thus of diminished culpability.

In the end, it is a satisfactory verdict for all involved. Even for Sigrid K., who traveled from Berlin to almost every day of the trial and almost always maintained her composure - even when Angelika described in detail in court how she and her ex-husband systematically tortured Anika and then disposed of her body. "For me, the verdict is fine," Sigrid says. Two or three more years didn't matter.

From Wilfried, Anika's mother even received a letter. However, she is not sure whether to keep it or throw it in the trash.

"Dear Mrs. K.," it says in the salutation, then follows, in scrawly script and awkward words, a statement about how sorry Wilfried is for all this.

"I will never forget Anika. She will always live on in my heart.

With love,

Wilfried."

»Hat er aber gemordet, so muss er sterben.«

- Immanuel Kant (1724-1804) deutscher Philosoph -

CHAPTER 6

The semitrailer

Lukasz is exhausted. The Polish truck driver has driven his heavy semitrailer all the way from Italy to Berlin, maneuvering 25 tons of steel across the German Federal Republic. Now he is stranded in the parking lot in front of the thyssenkrupp Schulte company on Friedrich-Krause-Ufer. There are delays in unloading his truck. Instead of today, Monday, he would not be able to get the load off the trailer until tomorrow, Tuesday. All the pleading and begging with the company's foreman hadn't helped, and Lukasz gave up. He would have to spend the night in Berlin. He had just treated himself to a kebab at a kebab stand for lunch. Now it was time to wait and kill time.

The stocky man makes himself comfortable in his well-cushioned driver's seat, lays his head back and closes his eyes. Christmas Eve is just a few days away. The main thing is that he manages to be back in Poland by then. His wife and son are already eagerly awaiting the return of the family man - always, but especially at Christmas time, the celebration of love and family.

While the man in his mid-thirties is preoccupied with his thoughts, he doesn't notice anyone approaching his semitrailer. When suddenly there is a banging on the driver's door, Lukasz is startled and looks out of the window into the face of a friendly-looking young man. The truck driver straightens up in his seat to reach the handle of the driver's door. Maybe it's a colleague who needs his help. Even as Lukasz opens the heavy door, the stranger's face contorts into a malevolent grimace. Lukasz looks down the barrel of a gun. Fear paralyzes him. He can neither react nor say anything. The stranger points the gun at his perplexed victim and climbs the steps to the cab. Lukasz is told to slide into the passenger seat while the man with the gun makes himself comfortable in the driver's seat. The Polish family man is breathing heavily; cold sweat now covers his entire body. With his eyes wide open and his hands raised, he watches the stranger. The stranger does not say a word, but the pointed weapon speaks a clear language. Lukasz is sure: no matter what this man is up to, he means business.

A short moment later, the loud bang of a gunshot shatters the tense silence in the cab. Lukasz slumps in the passenger seat. The bullet has seriously injured him - his hours-long struggle with death has begun.

Anis Ben Othman Amri was born in the Tunisian city of Tataouine on December 22, 1992. He is the youngest of nine children born to his parents Mustafa and Nour Amri. Shortly after the boy's birth, the extended family moves and from then on lives in the village of Oueslatia, which has 9,000 inhabitants. A stronghold of Salafism, an ultra-conservative, violent current of Islam.

The family of eleven lives in great poverty. To provide for their five daughters and four sons, mother Nour works as a domestic helper. Father Mustafa was an agricultural worker. After a serious accident, however, he is so physically limited that he can no longer do this job. From then on, he supplies stores with vegetables, which he transports from customer to customer in a donkey cart.

Religion is not a big issue in the Amri family. The women do not wear headscarves; there is no prayer. Anis is a normal teenager who parties, drinks alcohol and listens to pop music. At 15, he begins to rebel. The teenager drops out of school. Now and then he takes on odd jobs to keep his head above water. When he is short of money, he commits thefts. Until, to escape his dreary everyday life, the teenager begins to use drugs. At this point, he has already completely slipped away from his parents. Even his siblings can no longer exert a positive influence on the rebel.

2011 is the year of the Arab Spring. In the countries of North Africa and in several states of the Middle East, protests, uprisings, and revolutions are taking place against the totalitarian regimes that rule there. Amri, who has no prospects, is now 19 years old and goes on the run. He follows several young Tunisians who set out on the dangerous boat trip to the island of Lampedusa. On to a better life. It is April 5, 2011, when the Italian police register the illegal entry of the young Tunisian. However, he does not give his true year of birth, but 1994, which means he is considered an unaccompanied minor refugee who must be given special protection because of his young age.

The young man finds shelter in the home of a Catholic foundation in Belpasso, a town on the Italian island of Sicily. The youth is cared for there and they can attend a local school. But Amri's social behavior constantly leads to problems. He terrorizes his classmates and becomes violent towards them again and again. But it's not only at school that he gets into trouble. Anis doesn't let himself be restrained by anything or anyone. In his dormitory, he joins forces with four other rebellious youths. Together they protest. They are given bad food, not given enough cigarettes, no alcohol, and the length of the asylum procedure is unreasonable.

The caretakers in the home have understanding for the young people. Each of their charges has his or her own, often sad, story, and the teenagers are usually traumatized. When frustration is added to the mix, it is not uncommon for violence to erupt. But the staff at the home have nothing to counter the destructive rage that bursts out of Amri and his gang. On October 22, 2011, the five youths escalate to full-scale violence. They set fire to several rooms in the home and injure one of the caretakers with blows, punches, and kicks. This results in property damage of 30,000 euros.

Barely a year has passed since his escape when 19-year-old Anis is sentenced in a court case to four years' imprisonment for the incident at the home, which he is serving in a prison in the city of Catania. Until his release in May 2015, he is transferred twice to other detention centers because the convicted young man cannot control his aggression. He threatens and harasses his fellow inmates until they start fighting with him. He also trashes his cell and attacks the prison staff. Amri threatens one of his fellow inmates, who belongs to Christianity, full of hate: "I'll chop your head off!" As a result, the aggressive prisoner is under special surveillance.

After his release, the prison authorities report in detail on Anis's time in prison to the Strategic Counterterrorism Analysis Committee. Prison staff fear that the former inmate may become radicalized, as he openly sympathized with the ideas of Islamist terrorism during his time in prison.

The Italian city of Caltanissetta is home to the center for the identification and expulsion of illegal refugees. After his release from prison, Anis Amri arrives here. He is supposed to leave the country and return to Tunisia. But the countries' bureaucracy prevents his deportation. The Italian authorities claim that the Tunisian government has told them that the refugee is not from Tunisia and that they cannot issue any identification documents. And these would be however compellingly necessary for the deportation.

However, the Tunisian consulate in Palermo had already issued a birth certificate for Anis Amri in June 2011 and had also forwarded it to the relevant Italian authorities. Although the identity of the refugee was thus established beyond doubt, the Italians did not initiate deportation. Of course, no one can suspect it at this point, but this omission is the beginning of a disaster.

Amri hangs in the air, between states, between jurisdictions. He does not know what to do next. On June 17, 2015, he moves out of the "Center for the Identification and Expulsion of Illegal Refugees." The Italian authorities had given him seven days to leave the country, wherever.

But the Italian Information and Internal Security Agency is not letting the illegal refugee out of their sight for the time being, despite - or perhaps because of - the request to leave. They are certain: Amri, who is now classified as a radical Islamist, is trying to gain a foothold in the Italian jihadist scene. Followers of this scene believe it is their religious duty to defend Islam violently against infidels and Muslims of other persuasions. But a breakdown occurs in the surveillance of Anis Amri. The security forces lose sight of him. They have no choice but to enter all the information they have gathered into the Schengen Information System, or SIS, and put him on the wanted list.

The coming days and months in the 23-year-old's life seem to blur into one another. He remains in the so-called Schengen area; checks on persons at the borders of the associated countries do not take place. Amri decides to enter Switzerland - illegally. There, the authorities have no chance of catching or registering him. The Tunisian is hiding underground. His motto is to avoid attracting attention. Because it is already clear to him that he has an important mission.

It is later assumed that the young man contacted the Salafists in Switzerland. It is also suspected that these men supported Anis and established the connection to the Salafist scene in Germany. Anis' next goal was clear: To enter the German Federal Republic.

In 2015 and 2016, the Europe-wide refugee crisis reached its peak. More than a million refugees, migrants and other people seeking protection make their way to Central Europe from their unsafe, sometimes poor countries. Amri is taking advantage of the flight of these desperate people. It is the warm summer of 2015 when Anis also enters Germany. With his Tunisian passport in his pocket, he reports to the police station in Freiburg-Nord. However, Amri has no intention of revealing his true identity to the officers. He claims not to have a passport. His name is Anis "Amir" instead of "Amri. And he also fibs about his date of birth. He comes directly from Tunisia and wants to apply for asylum in Germany.

As with all other asylum seekers, the officials enter the young Tunisian's data into the Schengen Information System. Because of the misspelling of the man's name, the SIS cannot warn the authorities about the refugee, so the Tunisian received a so-called BüMA: a certificate of registration as an asylum seeker. With the important document in his pocket, Anis is supposed to make his way to the initial reception facility in Karlsruhe. At the same time, however, the officials initiate an investigation into the unauthorized entry into the German Federal Republic. Only a few days later, the officials discontinue the proceedings. Anis never arrived in Karlsruhe. No one knows where the fugitive is now. He is put on report for a residence investigation.

At this point, Amri is already in Berlin. Here he reports to a reception center again. He now calls himself

"Mohammad Hassan" and is again issued a BüMA. After some back and forth - many of the reception facilities for refugees are already full - "Mohammad" is stranded in a refugee shelter in the district of Kleve. There is still a small living space for the young man in Emmerich.

It is the end of October 2015, when the foreigners' authority turns to the police with concern. They report that the room neighbor of "Mohammed Hassan" made a disturbing discovery on the refugee's cell phone: a photo in which several men dressed in black posed with Kalashnikovs and hand grenades. Officials recognize the possible seriousness of the situation and initiate a procedure to check whether the picture has a possible Islamist background. What they fauk in doing, however, is to connect "Mohammad Hassan" with the known Islamist threat Anis Amri.

The latter is traveling without hindrance across the German Federal Republic, applying for asylum under at least fourteen different identities in different cities and having his social benefits paid out in each case. Under the alias "Ahmed Almasri," the terror sympathizer lives and resides in the North Rhine-Westphalian city of Oberhausen until March 2016.

Amri contacts the Salafist-jihadist network. The main figure in this network is Abu Walaa, a native of Iraq who lives in Hildesheim, Lower Saxony. The latter founded the "German-speaking Islamkreis Hildesheim e.V." in 2012. But Walaa does not only use this platform to spread his hate sermons. He also uses YouTube, Facebook, and Telegram to spread his thoughts of rage and destruction under the guise of peaceful Islam. His actions have not gone unnoticed by the security authorities, who have classified the hate preacher as a dangerous person. He is now under special surveillance. After years of observation by the Office for the Protection of the Constitution, it is clear that Abu Walaa plays a central role in recruiting fighters in Germany for IS, the Islamic State. And his recruitment network has stretched its tentacle-like arms to nearly every major city in Germany.

German heir Boban Simeonovic, alias Abdurrahman, also occupies an important role in the network at this point. He operates out of Dortmund in North Rhine-Westphalia. The Office of the Attorney General will later describe his tasks as follows: "To teach like-minded people and those willing to leave the country radical Islamic content in addition to the Arabic language. The lessons served to create the ideological and linguistic foundations for future activity with 'IS,' especially for participation in combat operations." Amri comes to Dortmund from time to time and stays with Simeonovic during this period. Through him, Anis also occasionally gets the opportunity to perform as a prayer leader in various Dortmund mosques. Due to the connection to Simeonovic, Anis

Amri is now also classified as a "danger to the county of North Rhine-Westphalia".

As early as the summer of 2015, a small, secret group is meeting in the mosque of the "German-speaking Islam Circle Hildesheim e.V.". Anis Amri is also among the participants of the meetings. The men discuss the possibility of carrying out an Islamist terrorist attack in Germany as well. Although Amri is being trained to fight in Syria, he likes the idea of a suicide attack in Germany so much that he decides against leaving the country.

At the same time, a preliminary investigation is underway against Abu Walaa. As part of this investigation, the North Rhine-Westphalia State Criminal Police Office tries to infiltrate an informant into Walaa's network - with success. On November 19, 2015, the informant reported to the LKA that he had come across a young man calling himself Anis during his undercover investigations. He said that he wanted to "do something" in Germany. Only a week later, the informant informs the LKA (State Criminal Investigation Office) that Anis claims to be able to get a Kalashnikov "without any problems in Naples". Another week later, the informant gets more specific: Anis wants to obtain a Kalashnikov in Paris. With this weapon, he plans to carry out a terrorist attack in Germany.

Following the informant's tips, the public prosecutor initiates a surveillance of Anis Amri's telecommunications

(TKÜ). In May 2016, however, the interception is discontinued because it is no longer legally permissible. Walaa and four of his accomplices are arrested on November 8, 2016, for running a "Salafist-jihadist IS recruitment network." Anis, however, plays only a minor role in the investigation against Walaa. No concrete indications emerged during the course of the TKÜ that would have authorized the security authorities to arrest Amri. He is considered a contact person but not a suspect, only a marginal figure - a serious misjudgment.

Berlin, Charlottenburg district. It is December 19, 2016, Christmas time. On Breitscheidplatz near the Memorial Church, built between 1891 and 1895 to commemorate Emperor Wilhelm I, hustle and bustle prevails. Numerous small wooden stalls form a Christmas market that invite to linger, browse for Christmas gifts, and enjoy a cup of hot mulled wine. Christmas classics resound from loudspeakers and the cool winter air is filled with the scent of roasted almonds, candied apples, and cotton candy. Smaller and larger groups of families and friends stroll from one beautifully winter-decorated Christmas booth to another. They chat and laugh. Most of them are already on Christmas vacation and in just a few days Christmas Eve will be upon them. Good food, time with loved ones, colorfully wrapped presents. The mood of the visitors is exuberant.

Anis Amri sits in the cab of the hijacked 40-ton truck and circles the bustling crowd. Next to him in the passenger seat is Lukasz, who is still wrestling with death. With every heavy breath the truck driver takes, a piece of his life force escapes. Amri appears unimpressed by the dying man beside him. With his left hand on the wheel, he fingers his cell phone out of his pocket with his right hand. Activates the camera app, set it to selfie mode. A sly smile, a touch of the red button on the display, done. With one eye half-heartedly fixed on the traffic ahead, he sends the picture he has just taken to one of his fellow believers and types a message after it: "My brother, all is well, God willing. I'm in the car now, pray for me my brother, pray for me." He then slides his cell phone back into his pocket.

Around 8:00 p.m., Amri steers the black tractor-trailer toward the Christmas market from Kantstraße. From one second to the next, the pre-Christmas atmosphere is shattered by bursting wood, screeching tires, the shattering glass of the truck's windshield and the panicked shouts of visitors. Lukasz's weakened body is no longer able to withstand the powerful impact. He loses the desperate fight against death.

When the 40-ton truck comes to a halt after 80 meters, there is an eerie silence for a few ghostly seconds before a storm of loud groans, cries of pain and cries for help break loose. Breitscheidplatz now resembles a battlefield of rubble, injured people, and corpses.

The assassin, who to his astonishment survives his terrorist attack, decides within a few seconds. He tears open the door of the driver's cab, rushes down the boarding ramps and runs away. At 8:02 p.m., the first frantic emergency calls are received by the police and fire department. A witness reports that he is chasing the fleeing assassin. He kept the officers up to date by cell phone until he lost sight of the perpetrator at the Siegessäule (victory column). But the police officers who rushed to the scene managed to arrest the man they were chasing. A sigh of relief. The murderer is caught. An asylum seeker from Pakistan.

A few hours later, however, the man is released. He is not the assassin from Breitscheidplatz. When the officials come to this realization, a shock runs through them. This mistaken arrest of an innocent man has led to the real assassin being able to make his escape undisturbed. God knows where he is now! In the belief that the Pakistani was the perpetrator, an important security measure did not come into effect: in the case of alleged Islamist attacks, it is stipulated that all people classified as Islamist threats must be visited at their known whereabouts.

The fact that this concept was not implemented is convenient for Anis Amri. The armed perpetrator can walk calmly to his apartment on Freienwalderstrasse. Once there, he hastily changes his clothes and packs a backpack with a few belongings. He then hurriedly leaves his accommodation. While the stunned population tries to comprehend the incomprehensible, the murderer mingles with them undetected. He boards subways and buses until he leaves the capital behind forever.

One day after the attack, the truck is examined by forensics. In the footwell of the cab, they find Amri's wallet and cell phone. And in the truck's radiator grille, forensics also find another cell phone belonging to the assassin. It is a mystery how the cell phone could have gotten there. But that is now irrelevant, the security authorities now know: Anis Amri is their wanted man! A Europe-wide manhunt for the attacker is launched.

The Tunisian, however, already left the country. He flees by bus and train from Berlin to the Netherlands, and from there to France, until he finally arrives in Italy. He knows there is no escape for him. The whole world is looking for him. Sooner or later, they would find him. He was not supposed to survive the attack. All that is left for him is to flee headlong and without a plan.

Italy, Sesto San Giovanni. It is one day before Christmas Eve, when on December 23, 2016, at 3:00 am, two police officers notice a young foreigner. He bears a resemblance to the wanted assassin from Breitscheidplatz. They decide to conduct a routine ID check. The patrolmen approach the unknown man and address him, "Passport? ID card?"

The foreigner takes his backpack off his back, opens it and rummages inside. In the next moment, one of the policemen notices a black object in the hand of his counterpart. But before he realizes what this black object is, he already sees a bright flash. A loud bang breaks the silence of the night. Then a burning pain in his shoulder. The wounded policeman goes down. His colleague recognizes the situation, pulls his gun out of the holster in a flash and points it at the attacker. He takes aim. A loud bang and the bright light of the muzzle flash. Anis Amri slumps on the wet asphalt, which soon turns blood-red. The killer's escape is over. He is dead.

Anna and Georgiy Bagratuni, Sebastian Berlin, Nada Cizmar, Fabrizia Di Lorenzo, Dalia Elyakim, Christoph Herrlich, Klaus Jacob, Angelika Klösters, Dorit Krebs and Peter Völker are murdered in the Islamist terrorist attack at Breitscheidplatz. Only the truck's automatic emergency braking system (ANB), which Amri did not consider when planning his attack, prevented more innocent people from being murdered. The ANB triggered after the tractor-trailer hit the first Christmas stalls.

Fifty-five people were injured in the attack, some of them seriously. And some of the emergency personnel at the scene, firefighters, and police officers, also suffer severe trauma in this operation, which will accompany them for many years to come.

One day after the terrible terrorist attack, an eerie silence reigns over Breitscheidplatz. The sky is dark and cloudy. It seems as if the ether joins in the grief and bewilderment of the people. Rain pelts the Christmas market; or rather, what's left of it. The debris of the Christmas stalls is cleared away. The wooden shacks that were not damaged have closed their crates. Red and white flagging tape blocks off the entrance. Women, men, and children, old and young, of every nationality and creed, have come with flowers and candles. Heavily armed policemen accept the gifts at the barrier; lay the flowers for the mourners and light the candles until a sea of lights has been created.

Cold wind whips against the guests on the church forecourt. They have come to pray for the dead, injured and their families in a funeral service at the Memorial Church. Most of the affected families, including Lukasz's family did not make it here today. The shock and pain of the loss that came upon them yesterday, without any warning, is too great.

Slowly and deliberately, people stream into the Memorial Church, among them high-ranking politicians. The guests shiver as they take their seats in the cold, hard pews. Cold, where actually a comfortably warm Christmas mood should prevail. "How must the families feel right now who have lost their loved ones or are worried about their seriously injured relatives?" may be going through the minds of one or the other.

In a speech, German Chancellor Angela Merkel, dressed all in mourning black, speaks of courage to the population: “We don’t want to live with the fear of evil paralyzing us. Even if it is difficult in these hours. We will find the strength for life as we want to live it in Germany: free, together and open.”

Whether the people affected by this attack will also find the strength for life afterwards, no one can say on this day.

The small rascals are locked up, the big ones one salutes to.

- Swabian saying -

CHAPTER 7

Fine feathers make fine birds

It is 1849, and while Guiseppe Mazzini proclaims the Roman Republic in the Papal States, the revolution that began in March 1848 continues to keep the population of the German Confederation in suspense.

In the midst of all this political unrest, Friedrich-Wilhelm Voigt was born on February 13, 1849, in Tilsit, East Prussia. His father, Johann Carl Christian Voigt, a master shoemaker, was fencing under the rule of Emperor Wilhelm I in Baden at the time.

Participation in military campaigns is something of a tradition in the Voigt family. Frederick-Wilhelm's grandfathers participated in the campaigns from 1813 to 1815. The boy also developed a liking for the military at an early age, not least because it was common practice in his hometown of Tilsit for a boy to start playing soldier as soon as he could walk. In addition, the Voigt family's apartment resides in a favorable location, directly opposite the barracks of the 1st Lithuanian Dragoon Regiment. Thus, it happens that between Friedrich-Wilhelm and the respective crew of the regiment a friendly contact is established which enables him to gain service knowledge when he is still a boy. The family looks to Frederick-Wilhelm's future with confidence, hoping he can use the army as a springboard to attain a respected civil service position.

Crucial to the boy's development above all is his "Uncle Patzig," the first husband of a sister of Friedrich-Wilhelm's mother. This uncle, a mechanic by trade and also a man of much knowledge, teaches his nephew reading, arithmetic and writing even before he enters school, which gives Friedrich-Wilhelm a considerable advantage over his classmates when he enters the local, three-grade town school in 1855. In 1858, he transfers to the secondary school.

Until then, the growing child's life seems to be characterized by prosperity, but this changes abruptly when Friedrich-Wilhelm reaches adolescence. One of the triggers for this is the recurring domestic violence of his father, who, after the early death of Uncle Patzig, develops an affinity for gambling and is regularly ripped off by other gamblers. Although this causes the family's fortune to dwindle from time to time and threatens to ruin their existence, the father cannot be dissuaded from his passion; much more, the family tries to keep their precarious financial situation hidden from the outside world as best they can.

To escape the "domestic scenes," as Friedrich-Wilhelm titles the tense family idyll, he often leaves the parental home secretly and seeks shelter with his relatives in Königsberg, 110 kilometers away. During these excursions, he repeatedly came into conflict with law enforcement officers, until he was caught stealing for the first time at the age of 14 and was sentenced to two weeks in prison by the Tilsit District Court in 1863.

Since he now had a criminal record, Friedrich-Wilhelm was not allowed to continue attending school and had to find an alternative - which he found in his father's profession. As a journeyman shoemaker, Friedrich-Wilhelm also undertakes years of travel, which take him through large parts of Pomerania and Brandenburg. However, even during these adventures he is unable to tear himself away from his criminal activities. In 1867, at the age of 18, he is sentenced to twelve years in prison for forging documents.

After serving his sentence, Friedrich-Wilhelm Voigt was not even free for a year before he committed document forgery again in 1889 and shortly afterwards even a robbery: with a crowbar he plundered the court treasury in the Prussian district of Wongrowitz. This offense landed him in prison "for grand larceny" - this time for fifteen years.

When Voigt served his last prison sentence for the time being in 1906, the native of Tilsit was already 57 years old and had spent more than half of his life behind bars.

Now, however, Friedrich-Wilhelm intends to leave his old life behind and earn his money in an "honest way". To do this, he doesn't even want to try to find a job in the German Reich, but instead wants to make a new start in Austria-Hungary or Russia. There is only one problem: Voigt needs a passport for his plan, but he is denied one because of his criminal record.

Therefore, he first moves to Wismar in Mecklenburg, where he tries his luck with the court shoemaker Hillbrecht. Soon, however, he is expelled from the Duchy of Mecklenburg-Schwerin and finally arrives in Berlin-Rixdorf, where his sister Bertha gives him shelter in her apartment. There he even found work in the felt shoe factory Albert Viereck, but the authorities kept a constant eye on him. As a result, in August 1906 the police issued Voigt a ban on staying in the greater Berlin area "as a precaution". This put an end to the shoemaker's dream of "continuing to work honestly" and then perhaps one day setting up a shoe store in Bernau for the Wismar court supplier.

Nevertheless, Voigt defied the residence ban and stayed as a “sleeping boy” in unregistered lodgings in Berlin-Friedrichshain near the Silesian train station. At first, he retained his job in the shoe factory, but due to his illegal status he had no future prospects there and resigned at the beginning of October 1906.

Since the authorities still refused to give him an identity card, Voigt devised a perfidious plan to gain possession of such a document: He wants to disguise himself as a captain and march into the rooms of an authority with some soldiers in tow. There, he wants to gain power over the authorities and use a pretext to scam the necessary form to end his illegal residence status. The “Köpenickiade” is born.

In devising his scheme, the shoemaker is most inspired by writer Heinrich Von Kleist, who impressively describes his campaign against the authorities in his novella “Michael Kohlhaas”. Since Voigt also feels betrayed by justice, he wants to create a memorial with his rogue play. He buys a somewhat shabby, but at the same time well-preserved, captain’s uniform from the junk dealer Bertold Remlinger in Potsdam.

He chose the town hall in Köpenick as the setting, not because of any special historical background, but because the town seems to him to be easiest to reach from his hideout by train. And there is another reason for the choice of the town hall, because Voigt is by no means merely interested in regaining his passport. Since he, as a newly unemployed man, is threatened with running out of money, he wants to raid the safe in the Köpenick town hall. It is said to contain two million marks.

But Voigt's coup, against his knowledge, is doomed to failure before it has even begun - because passports are not issued in a town hall, but at the district administration office.

So as not to run the risk of being observed in his disguise by other residents of the house and possibly being exposed, Voigt puts on the ankle-length, gray captain's uniform with the blue collar, the thick buttons, and the white belt with golden buckle in his apartment early in the morning of October 16, 1906 and steps out onto the deserted street at around 3:30 am.

First, Voigt takes the 4:00 a.m. train to Köpenick at the Schlesischer Bahnhof to take stock of the situation there. The magnificent town hall, a brick castle with a Gothic-style clock tower completed in 1905, is located in the center of Köpenick's old town, which was built in the 12th century and sits on an island between the Dahme and Spree rivers.

After gathering all the information, the fake captain returns to Berlin around six o'clock. He stays there for a few hours and then takes a cab to Wedding, a district of

Berlin, where he has lunch in a garden restaurant. On the way there, Voigt meets a major of the airship division and for a few minutes, fears for his cover. However, the major does not seem to notice anything unusual. The disguise works.

After lunch, the fake captain vagabonds around Seestraße for some time until he finally meets a troop of Fusiliers of the Guards Fusilier Regiment, nicknamed "Maybugs", in the connecting street Sylterstraße. Voigt seizes the opportunity and orders the company, in a strong East Prussian accent, to "Halt!". The corporal stands at attention and makes the prescribed report to the false captain about the "where from" and "where to". According to the report, his four-man unit was on its way back to the barracks from guard duty at the military swimming pool at Plötzensee. Voigt informs the assembled squad in a sharp tone that they are not allowed to march to the barracks now, as they would be ordered by him to another service by higher command. He then instructs the corporal to summon a second squad of relieved guardsmen from the 4th Guards Regiment on foot, which the latter does without hesitation.

When the second guard team has also approached and reported to their leader Voigt, the false captain orders the first guard commander to the commander of the whole, lets him rank the team and orders the second commander to the end of the squad. Then Voigt gives the order to march off.

Since he had allegedly not succeeded in "requisitioning" motor vehicles, the false captain led his troop, now eleven strong, to Putlitzstraße station and bought tickets for the Berlin light rail, which took them in the direction of Köpenick. At a stopover in Rummelsburg, Voigt buys the soldiers a beer since they had not returned to the barracks after their guard duty and thus had no opportunity to refresh themselves; he himself treats himself to a cognac for 25 pfennigs. When the train then arrives in Köpenick in the early afternoon, the false captain presses a mark into the hand of each of his men and lets them have lunch in the station restaurant for fifteen minutes while he strolls up and down the corridor.

At the appointed time, Voigt summons the team back to the front of the station building to complete a duty roster for the upcoming coup at the town hall. The fake captain declares that he will "arrest the mayor and perhaps other gentlemen," then has the soldiers fix bayonets to remind them that they are "not commanded for pleasure, but for duty." He does not consider instructions for the treatment of individuals necessary, since experience has taught him that anyone who has served even one year knows how to treat an arrestee.

Arriving at the town hall, Voigt first sets up posts around the building. He decreed that the "cockchafers" should man the three portals of the town hall with one sentry each. Voigt orders an off-duty local gendarme, who is loitering on the front steps, to "return to duty immediately" and to assist the troop leader, to whom he gives command of the town hall.

Voigt chooses all his orders and commands with such calmness and composure that no one even suspects that the entire action could be faked. And the longer his plan seems to work, the more the false captain, who had to give in and hide from the authorities his entire life, grows into his role.

Before he goes inside the town hall, Voigt explicitly tells his protégés that no one is allowed to leave or enter the town hall without his order. At about 3:30 p.m., with six grenadiers of the 4th Guards Regiment and a fusilier in tow, he marches to the second floor, directly to the office of the chief town clerk, Rosenkranz.

When the fake captain opens the door, Rosenkranz is sitting behind his desk, calmly processing papers. Voigt tells him to get ready to leave immediately, as Voigt has orders to take him to the Neue Wache in Berlin. Rosenkranz follows the instructions without resistance, whereupon the false captain goes to the adjoining study of the mayor of Köpenick, Dr. Georg Langerhans. The mayor is initially surprised by the visit of the entourage, but then jumps up in horror when he recognizes the rank of the false captain. The latter informs him that he has to arrest him "by the highest order" and take him to the Neue Wache in Berlin.

The flabbergasted Dr. Langerhans inquires about the reason for his arrest, whereupon Voigt tries to brush him off: he himself does not know the exact reason and the mayor would find out everything "there". But Dr. Langerhans does not let up and demands that the captain show him some "official document" that legitimizes his arrest. Voigt barks that his legitimation is his soldiers and threatens the rebellious man with imprisonment if he continues to defy his majesty's orders. The mayor surrenders to his fate.

To add further power to his authority, Voigt orders two of his soldiers to stand guard at the mayor's side while he himself goes to the cashier's room on the first floor. On his way there, Voigt makes a detour to the office of police inspector Jäckel, whom he finds asleep in his armchair. After Voigt wakes him up, the false captain inquires whether Jäckel is paid by the city of Köpenick to sit around and slumber. He should have the goodness to go out to ensure the necessary order on the streets in front of the town hall. The police inspector immediately obeys the order of the "captain," but returns a few minutes later, puzzled and equally distraught. He was refused exit, he stammers, and asks the false captain to give him leave of absence. Since Voigt feels this is urgently needed, he grants the man his leave, whereupon he disappears to take a bath.

In the cashier's room, Voigt confronts Rendant von Wiltburg with a fait accompli: the mayor of the city of Köpenick is under arrest and he, the captain, has the power of command over the city hall. Voigt instructs the treasurer to make the cash balance and explains to him that he must confiscate the stock of the city treasury due to "irregularities in the sewerage works currently being carried out in Köpenick".

After the treasurer has meticulously counted and recalculated the money, which has to be fetched from the local post office, among other places, exactly 4,002 marks and 37 pfennigs end up in small bags, which the false captain has fetched and sealed. Voigt signs a receipt requested by the governor with the name of his last prison governor, "von Mahlzahn", and the addition "H.i.1.G.R." - Captain in the 1st Guards Regiment. Finally, Voigt had his prisoners brought to Berlin in hackney carriages; a soldier of the Guard Fusilier Regiment served as escort. Voigt himself stayed behind.

When the convoy arrived at the Neue Wache, they looked at confused faces. After all, no one there knows anything about an alleged military occupation of the town hall in Köpenick, including the arrest of the mayor.

Gradually, it dawns on those involved that they have fallen victim to a fraud. All attempts to track down the fake captain fail, however, because Voigt has long since made off with his loot. After completing his action, he had given the guards at the town hall money for beer, sausages and return tickets and ordered them to hold the fort for another half hour. Then he had gone to Köpenick station to return to Berlin on the next train. Before that, he had a glass of beer served to him in the station restaurant, which he emptied "in one go."

Once in Berlin, Voigt got rid of his uniform, stowed it in a cardboard box and bought a suit, coat, and hat from the best men's outfitter; he paid for the clothes with a thousand-mark bill. Then he resumes his old rank in civilian life and disappears into the hustle and bustle of the big city.

Meanwhile, news of the siege of the town hall in Köpenick spreads like wildfire, and soon the farce of the false captain is known far beyond the borders of the country. The day after the crime, the first picture postcards and caricatures can already be purchased, flyers with special reports are distributed on the streets.

The East Prussian authoritarian state becomes a worldwide public laughingstock: "The whole of Germany is laughing at this," newspapers headline gloatingly on the front page. Even Emperor Wilhelm II is said to have called

Voigt a "genius". Nevertheless, the emperor was no longer willing to put up with the blasphemies and, without further ado, offered a high reward for the capture of the villain.

After only a few days, the authorities receive a decisive clue. A scoundrel named Kallenberg reports that his former cellmate Friedrich-Wilhelm Voigt once confided in him that he was planning such a coup as soon as he was released.

When the police present a photo of Voigt from his criminal file to the staff of the Köpenick city hall, they immediately recognize him. Thus, the identity of the false captain is finally clarified, and Kallenberg is richer by a whopping 3000 marks. But one question remains unsolved: Where is the guy?

He can't have completely vanished into thin air. His uniform is found by passers-by on the grounds of Berlin Tempelhof Airport, but even this does not lead the police to the desired success. There is still no trace of the false captain.

When the police finally showed up at Voigt's sister's home in Rixdorf, where Voigt was still registered, the woman proved to be extremely cooperative. She provided the policemen with the address to Voigt's hideout - a direct hit that the police could hardly believe. On the morning of October 26, 1906, ten days after his racket, Voigt is arrested. Five weeks later, on December 1, 1906, the false captain stands trial before the Third Criminal Chamber of District Court II in Berlin on charges of unauthorized exercise of a public office, unauthorized wearing of a uniform, fraud, forgery of documents, and unlawful deprivation of liberty.

During the trial, which is accompanied by journalists from all over the world, it turns out that Voigt was never in the army and acquired his military knowledge in early childhood. So how had he managed to deceive every member of the "Köpenickiade"? Even Mayor Dr. Georg Langerhans, an inveterate reserve officer, had not noticed that the fake captain was, firstly, too old - the age limit for the rank of "captain" at that time was 56, but Voigt was already 57 -, secondly, spoke a strong dialect, and, moreover, his uniform had several flaws, such as a false cockade on his cap.

The reason for the success of his charade was Voigt's self-confident appearance and the dashing tone with which he barked the commands. In retrospect, all involved can consider themselves lucky that it remained at a simple arrest, because the soldiers testify in court that they would have used their bayonets and firearms without hesitation if they had been instructed to do so by Voigt.

The Prussian military as well as the imperial authorities hoped that the trial and resulting verdict would cast a bad light on Voigt and deter possible imitators of the deed, but far from it. The court sentenced the shoemaker to a "mere" four years in prison in the Tegel correctional facility. None of his civil rights, such as the right to vote, to be elected himself, or the right to hold public office, e.g., serving as a juror in court, were taken away from him - which is very unusual in view of his criminal record.

As a mitigating factor, the court allows the fact that Voigt "after serving his last sentence had made serious and successful efforts to earn his living honestly and was well on the way to becoming a useful member of civil society."

After his early release from prison in 1908, Voigt rose to media stardom. Just one day later, he immortalized his bright voice in East Prussian dialect for 200 marks on an almost three-minute gramophone recording, in which he spoke, among other things, about his thoughts during his imprisonment and addressed words of thanks to his admirers:

"Ladies and gentlemen,

if I do not speak to you publicly as a person, but only through my voice, I believe myself obliged to express my deepest gratitude for the many proofs which you have expressed to me in this or that form during the last difficult life. [...] The lively expressions of gratitude that have come to me from all sides are a beautiful gift that you have given me in my old age. I am well aware of the value of these expressions.

[...] the longing in me to walk as a free man among free men grew ever greater. I have now become free - but I wish and pray that God may protect me from becoming free once again. Now I greet you myself from here and want to hold on to the hope that it will still be granted to me [...] to express in freer and more comprehensive speech what my life has taught me and how I have become poor in my life sometimes, but also rich sometimes - even if not in possessions and goods - than it is possible in this pressed and bound form.

And now I ask you to continue to hold me in good memory. It is gratifying and uplifting to know and feel that thousands of hearts are ready to lift, bear and forgive. As far as the external circumstances of my dismissal are concerned, the final verdict has not yet been pronounced. Good things take time!

With heartfelt greetings and old joys, Wilhelm Voigt".

Again and again, he was offered horrendous sums for an exclusive story or had to pose for a photo in his captain's uniform. In 1909, the fuss about his person took on such proportions that Voigt even had autograph cards printed, which he published at the same time as his biography " How I Became Captain of Köpenick".

As his fame gradually faded, Voigt moved to Luxembourg, where he worked mainly as a waiter and shoemaker. Thanks to his popularity, however, he was able to achieve a certain prosperity and bought a two-seater French Lacoste & Battman, making him one of the first owners of an automobile in the Grand Duchy of Luxembourg.

During the First World War, the false captain once again comes into conflict with the Prussian military. German troops take him into custody in his new home and interrogate him. The lieutenant in charge of this operation notes in his diary, “It remains puzzling to me how this pathetic man could once shake all of Prussia.”

Friedrich-Wilhelm Voigt spent the last years of his life in solitude and seclusion in a house on the Rue du Fort Neipperg. On January 3, 1922, as a result of lung disease, he died at the age of 72. H was completely impoverished due to the war and inflation

At his funeral in the Liebfrauen cemetery in the Luxembourg district of Limpertsberg, the funeral procession encountered a squad of French soldiers. When the squad leader inquires about the name of the deceased, he is answered: “Le Capitaine de Coepenick” - “The Captain of Köpenick”.

Assuming that a real captain is being laid to rest, the officer orders his men to assume posture and salute to pay their last respects to the dead "Capitaine."

To this day, the charade of Friedrich-Wilhelm Voigt remains a German myth. His grave, however, has become a place of pilgrimage, most recently due to Carl Zuckermayer's tragicomedy: "Der Hauptmann von Köpenick - ein deutsches Märchen" (The Captain of Köpenick - A German Fairy Tale).

The story has served as a model for numerous books, films, songs, and plays. Millions of viewers flocked to the cinemas in the early fifties when Heinz Rühmann marched across the screen in the role of Friedrich-Wilhelm Voigt.

Today, at the town hall in Köpenick, a life-size bronze statue by artist Spartak Babajan, as well as a permanent exhibition inside the building, commemorates the former shoemaker whose rogue prank exposed and embarrassed Kaiser Wilhelm and his unchallenged, Prussian authoritarian state.

Whatever punishment is inflicted on me will be less cruel than the memory of my crime.

- Jean-Jacques Rousseau (1712-1778),
writer, philosopher, and leading figure
of the French Revolution -

CHAPTER 8

A nameless tombstone

(Harmke Horst / FINDING instead of SEARCHING - the Mantrailing Podcast)

It is a wonderfully warm summer day in June 2005. A popular fishing and bathing lake north of the A2 in Lower Saxony is bustling with activity. The lake is not only a popular excursion destination for many families but is also a popular destination for truck drivers due to its proximity to the highway. The drivers enjoy their short break away from the stuffy and noisy highway to the fullest. The lake is also a popular destination for fishermen. Just like today, they often sit for hours, or even overnight, at the water's edge with their fishing rods, hoping to make their best catch. In doing so, they indulge in pure relaxation in a natural setting. They gaze for hours at a still and quiet lake.

Among many other people, two friendly families are enjoying their time spent together in the fresh air on this summery day. The children play mindlessly near the shore. The family dog Oscar is extensively sniffing his way through the exciting surroundings. All these scents and smells are for him as for humans reading the current daily newspaper.

Oscar is just intensely sniffing a green-brown shrub when a gust of wind blows something extraordinarily exciting into his nose. The scent can't be far away. The dog picks up the scent and runs purposefully in the direction of the source of the smell. The four-legged friend almost runs by: Oscar brakes sharply, stretches his nose first to the right and then toward the ground. Suddenly he doesn't move from the spot. The dog's tail moves faster and faster and he starts digging frantically. At first, no one notices Oscar's little adventure, but after he doesn't want to leave his hole, he attracts the attention of the adults - and the hole.

Arriving at the excitedly pawing dog, the dog owner is hit by a terrible stench. It smells extremely unpleasantly of something decomposed. Disgusted, the man pulls his dog back by the collar - what kind of deceased animal has he dug up this time? But when Oscar disappears from the man's field of vision, he makes a discovery that gives him a sinking feeling in his stomach at first glance. A plastic bag is hastily buried in the sand. Cautiously the dog owner takes a glance into the dirty bag. The smell is hardly bearable now, but it is the sight that makes his blood run cold: Inside the bag, wrapped in a terrycloth towel, is the lifeless body of a small baby.

Quick-witted, the father grabs his children and takes them away from the beach. One of the witnesses immediately grabs his cell phone with a shaky hand, dials the number of the police and reports the gruesome find.

Schmidt, an experienced homicide investigator from Lower Saxony, has been with the Criminal Investigation Department for years. On this day he actually has time off and completely different plans. But when he receives a report of the discovery of a baby's body, he doesn't hesitate for long. He drives directly to the lake, to the place where the little corpse was deposited. Arriving at the actually so picturesque spot, he and his colleagues get a first rough overview of what is happening. The hot summer day doesn't make things any easier - the sun not only burns the officers' heads, but also makes the team sweat within a few minutes. An acrid smell quickly makes itself felt in the nostrils.

The idyllic lake atmosphere is no longer apparent, although the silence of everyone on site is almost as oppressive as the heat. Only the traffic roaring along the nearby highway creates a monotonous background hum. Carefully, so as not to destroy any trace, the officers open the plastic bag. Another bag from another supermarket emerges. The police officers then recognize the small body. Shaking his head, an officer steps aside. A cold shiver runs down Schmidt's spine. The baby is wrapped in a blood-soaked cloth. At first glance, investigators notice the cut on the infant's neck. Schmidt has seen a lot in his career, but a baby corpse is always a special challenge. When he assures the public that he will solve the crime, he has no idea how big and lengthy this challenge will be.

Professional divers comb the lake and the dense, already slightly dry shore in search of evidence. All potentially interesting objects around the dumping site are secured: among other things, the officers find a spoon soiled with sand, used handkerchiefs and some cigarette butts. There is no trace of a murder weapon.

The "Baby" homicide unit is set up. However, initial investigations by the CID do not yield any decisive clues to the baby's identity; an immediate, large-scale public search for the mother also comes to nothing. Neither does a search of doctors, especially gynecologists, pharmacies, and hospitals. Questioning of visitors and observation at the lake are not crowned with success either. The little one remains a sad mystery.

One morning, however, an angler came forward and the investigators sensed the first hot lead. The man claims to have been fishing at the lake with his friend at the end of June 2005. In the early afternoon, a chalk-pale woman with a bulging backpack scurried through the bushes. When the anglers approached the woman, however, she disappeared just as quickly as she had arrived. The assumption that the mother of the infant had been at the lake was supported by a genetic examination of the cigarette butts. In addition, other witnesses report having seen the woman at the lake. Female DNA traces could also be secured on the plastic bag in which the newborn girl was wrapped. However, the comparison in the database did not produce a hit. Thus, it remains unclear who the mother is.

The autopsy of the infant reveals that the little girl was alive and perfectly healthy at birth. The baby was killed - immediately after she saw the light of day. The cause of death is obvious. Several cross-sections on the throat, which led to the child's bleeding to death, are detected by the forensic pathologist during his examination. Presumably, the birth - and at the same time the murder - took place only a few days before the body was found.

A few days after the autopsy, the unknown infant is buried in a children's cemetery near the place where the body was deposited, with great public participation. More than 200 citizens, including many children, take part in the moving funeral service. It is supposed to be a dignified farewell. The small chapel does not offer as much space as people want to participate; some mourners therefore even stand in front of the chapel. They pay their last respects to the unknown baby, deeply touched. The small white coffin is decorated with a colorful sea of flowers and cuddly toys. The people put up a gravestone. Where there is usually a name, "Unknown Baby" is engraved in the stone. The local kindergarten immediately agrees to take care of the grave in the future. Many candles shine brightly to bid farewell to the girl. There are more than moving pictures that can be seen in the media following the funeral and the funeral procession.

Even before the funeral, eye-catching advertisements are placed by the local funeral home. The burial of the baby's body is deliberately taking place in a way that is extremely effective in terms of media coverage. The investigators hope to lure the birth mother to the gravesite. However, without success. The search for the still unknown woman continues.

In the meantime, a sketch of the mother is being made on the basis of the witness statements. An initial comparison with the missing persons file does not yield a hit in this case. Finally, the picture is presented to the public. If the pregnancy had been concealed or repressed, no one from the mother's environment would miss a newborn - but perhaps they would recognize the woman herself. But all further clues and traces come to nothing. The high frequency of visitors, even from truck drivers pausing only briefly, does not make the search any easier either.

Despite the setbacks, Schmidt and his homicide squad do not give up, but resort to innovative investigative methods. Among other things, Schmidt seeks advice from a criminologist who has dealt extensively with the killing of babies and their mothers. She explains: "Most homicides are relationship crimes, the murderers of the babies from the family. Often it is unnoticed, repressed, or concealed pregnancies from which these babies originate. The perpetrators come from all social classes and have often experienced some form of psychological dependence on their families or partners.

At the end of 2005, the public was once again asked to help in a way that attracted a lot of media attention. In the well-known German television series "Aktenzeichen XY," in which callers can help solve criminal cases, the case is reported on December 8, 2005. A short film reenacts the facts ascertained up to that point. A reward is even offered for tips that lead to success. But unfortunately, even the numerous pieces of information received do not bring the investigators any decisive step further.

The next unusual and not yet widely used investigative approach that the CID officer considers, discusses with experts, and then implements is isotope analysis. This is a method often used as a last resort to identify an unidentified dead person. The officer has the bones and fingernails of the baby's corpse examined by special scientists who create what is known as an isotopic fingerprint. This examination may allow conclusions to be drawn about the circumstances of the person giving the sample. Put simply, it analyzes components that have been deposited in the person's body over the course of his or her life as a result of environmental influences and reveals, for example, where and when someone lived, or what was mainly eaten.

In the current case, the investigators hope that the isotopic analysis of the infant - based on the genetic similarity of mothers and their children - will equally lead to conclusions about the mother. And indeed, the scientists conclude that the mother may have lived in Russia and later in the northern German lowlands. This brings truck drivers back into the focus of the investigation - did someone perhaps drive the mother and baby to the lake? But this time, too, the investigations in this direction remain unsuccessful.

Four and a half years pass. The little girl may be nothing more than a bad memory for some by now, but Inspector Schmidt does not give up and once again dares to take a rather unusual investigative approach: special people tracking dogs, also called "mantrailers" in layman's terms. For the police of Lower Saxony, the "means of operation person tracking dog" is at this time still absolutely new. At a specialist conference of the LKA, Schmidt learns for the first time about this method, which has hardly been taken into account to date, and contacts the speakers.

The first dog-assisted search to locate the mother takes place at the lake a short time later, in November 2009. Since the police of Lower Saxony do not have person tracking dogs themselves at this time, dogs that are privately owned are used with their handlers.

People tracking dogs are trained to follow human traces even after a longer period of time. Unlike tracking dogs, which are guided by ground lesions, people-sniffing dogs look for the individual scent of a specific person. The individual odor is as unique as the fingerprint - every person thus smells different to the dog. In dogs, the nose as a primary organ is far more pronounced and larger than in humans. To find the scent trail of a specific person, the dog receives a reference scent of the person to be searched for in the form of a so-called olfactory article. In this case: traces of the mother's blood and odor particles from the plastic bag in which the baby's body was wrapped. The person-sniffing dog picks up the scent and stores this information in its olfactory brain. From then on, the dog compares this reference odor with the particles in its environment and tries to pick up and follow a matching scent trail.

The police meet the dog handlers and their person tracking dogs at the lake. Beforehand, the tactics of the operation are briefly discussed. Slight excitement spreads among all participants. Even the dogs show - in joyful expectation of the search - a tension of the whole body. Once at the starting point, the former place where the infant was deposited, the first dog is put on his working harness. The snap hook of the drag line audibly snaps into the D-ring of the harness. This connection between dog and human allows them to search safely in almost any environment. Nevertheless, busy sections are always blocked off later during the search to ensure the safety of all involved.

On this day, the people tracking dog succeeds in picking up a trail at the site where the dead infant was found. Led by the long drag line, the dog - with the lake at its back - walks in front. He pulls along more and more, and everyone hurries to keep up. After some time, however, the search is interrupted without further success.

People tracking dogs are trained to always find the freshest scent trail of the person to be searched, starting from the starting point. Thus, the reconstructed scent trail could also be a much fresher one than the one from the filing day. A difficult thought for Schmidt – because the longer there is no success in the investigation, the more the fear grows among the officers that the mother could kill a baby a second time.

At the beginning of 2010, another search is carried out with the person tracking dogs. In addition to the site where the body was found, this time the animals are also deployed at the gravesite of the anonymously buried girl. Here, the four-legged specialists can also pick up a scent matching the odor article. This trail leads to the parking lot and from there to the A2 in the direction of Hanover.

Even when a person gets into a vehicle – no matter on which seat – odor particles are swirled into the environment outside the vehicle, which can be traced even after a long time. The question investigators now ask is: at which exit did the car with the person they were looking for leave the highway? To determine this, the task forces take on each individual exit. Exit by exit, the people-sniffing dogs are set to find out where they pick up scent again. If a dog strikes, this is an indication that the person they are looking for has left the highway at that point.

Following this tactic, the search party moves further and further in the direction of the Hannover East interchange to the A7. The search then continues via Hamburg to Schleswig-Holstein. For investigator Schmidt, it is still an unusual search operation that extends over several days due to the long distance. Then the search is interrupted – for the time being.

A few weeks later, in March 2010, people tracking dogs are again deployed in a port city on the German Baltic coast. Among other things, they are on the move in the red-light district. The homicide squad suspects that the mother of the slain infant might be or have been in this area. The search proceeds rather sluggishly, as a known rocker group briefly interrupts the investigators' work there. But after the group learns the real reason for the search, they back off. But even then, no real hot lead can be found.

Following the deployment of the dogs, the investigators must evaluate the search for clues. The police officers are still unsure to what extent the trace reconstructed by the dogs can contribute to solving the crime. It would be more than spectacular if the trail led to success.

In early 2011 – over five years have passed since the baby was found. A lot has been done, the latest methods have been tried out, never given up, and yet the breakthrough in the manhunt happens rather by chance. A VW bus is stolen in a town in Lower Saxony in October 2010. It takes five months for the vehicle to turn up in the parking lot of an allotment garden. Forensic investigators are able to recover a cigarette butt in the ashtray and hand it over to the State Criminal Police Office for analysis. The workload at the LKA is high at this time and the analysis takes a long time – but then the hit. A match is found to the DNA pattern to the still unknown child mother of the baby body found in 2005. In addition, the parking lot where the car was found is only a few kilometers away from the scene of the lake.

In April 2011, the LKA informs the homicide squad about the trail hit. The surprise is great; hardly anyone expects such a hot lead after such a long time. The officers immediately start investigating: The vehicle is registered to a catering business, by which it is used as a company vehicle and thus driven by various people. The homicide squad begins to investigate at full speed in the vicinity of the catering business. The excitement in the homicide department "Baby" is rising. Is this finally the decisive lead? Again, witnesses are questioned and various women who work or have worked in the establishment are asked to provide a saliva sample. However, a 35-year-old woman does not show up at the appointed time. The officers become suspicious.

As the investigators pursue this lead ever more vehemently, the net around the woman tightens, and the situation seems hopeless for her, the wanted woman finally turns herself in to the police in May 2011. She called the police and stated that she was the murderer of the baby from the lake. After almost six years of intensive searching by the homicide squad, the child's mother is now arrested by the officers. After the arrest, the woman is interrogated several times. She confesses to having killed her baby in 2005 directly after birth by cutting her throat.

The parties involved are still in the process of digesting this information when the 35-year-old shocks the investigators again: she has recently given birth to a second girl. It was born in the bathtub. After a short period of unconsciousness, the baby was no longer alive – it had drowned in the bath water. Again, the mother wrapped the girl in a plastic bag and kept her at home. However, when the woman felt more and more harassed by the search efforts, she threw the dead girl into a nearby dumpster. The mother describes to investigators exactly where this dumpster is located.

While they are still questioning her, colleagues from the commission are sent to the spot. And indeed: in the middle of a huge pile of garbage it lies – the little dead girl. The suspect is taken into custody.

The life of the arrested mother had not always been easy, as she recounts during the trial. She came from a large family with a strong religious background. The family lives in Lower Saxony almost crammed together, considering the number of children, in a small apartment. The father calls the shots. Abuse and harassment were the order of the day. She did not experience love, but only fear of her family. Sexuality is never discussed. When the woman is threatened with forced marriage, she can no longer stand it at home. She flees.

In her new environment, the suspect lives a life that officially almost does not exist. She has no identity card, no health insurance, and no registration address. Allegedly, the woman does not dare to register anything, in fear that her family might find her. She keeps her head above water with odd jobs in betting shops or in the restaurant business, and sometimes she has no choice but to live on savings. For her environment she invents the most different stories about her past: Sometimes she was adopted in her childhood, another time she says that she was in a convent.

At the beginning of the trial, the suspect renews her confession. Many factors had contributed to the terrible deeds. She had suppressed her first pregnancy until the day of birth. Even with the onset of labour, she did not want to admit what was happening. The birth, which lasted almost a day, had been associated with great pain; the woman was completely alone. Due to some additional complications, the delivery had been almost unbearable. The woman felt trapped in a state of shock, in which the situation seemed completely unreal to her.

The baby girl is finally born in the bathroom in a breech position. She screams. And screams. And screams. The suspect can't take it anymore. She longs for silence. As if in a trance, she cuts the throat of the newborn girl with a kitchen knife. Then silence follows.

As the mother continues, she cites as another reason for her actions that the child was not wanted. She was completely distraught by the unplanned pregnancy.

After the murder, she wrapped the dead baby in a towel, packed it in several plastic bags, and hid the bundle in the closet. A few days later, she had her boyfriend drive her to the nearby lake - ostensibly to get some rest. There, she buried the small bundle in the sand with the help of a spoon.

From then on, the defendant repressed what had happened. She continued living as if nothing had happened. When she sees something about the crime in the media, she looks at it like a spectator, not like the perpetrator. Again and again, she drowns her thoughts about the event in alcohol.

The father of the first baby was involved with the suspect for years, although he already had a family. During the trial, he explained that he traveled a lot for work. After almost ten years of relationship, he finally separated from his family and moved in with the accused. He neither suspected nor realized that he was pregnant. Not even when it came to sex shortly before the delivery.

The second pregnancy a few years later was at first just as unwanted as the first, the woman says. But then she was looking forward to having the child. She met the father of the second baby during one of her part-time jobs in the restaurant business. Although the restaurateur also had a family, a long affair developed between the two. This man also testified not to have noticed anything about the pregnancy, although he also had sex with the defendant until shortly before the birth. She had only had a small bulge on her belly and when she denied being pregnant, he believed her.

During the trial, one of the defendant's lovers described her as a woman with two faces. Sometimes she would have faced him in a strange, almost befuddled state. Then she was completely lucid again; a woman who was completely resilient and who liked children very much. That this woman could kill a child, he would never have thought possible.

Further, it turns out in the trial that the accused woman had been pregnant a third time between the two known births - again by another man. In this pregnancy, however, a miscarriage had occurred after a few weeks.

Based on the statements, the whole life of the accused seems to be riddled with lies and constructs, it seems like a parallel world. The media-effective manhunts - like the phantom picture or the search with the person tracking dogs - the mother does not refer to herself at any time. She disappears when things get difficult, in her subconscious constantly with death as her companion. She simply felt abandoned by the girls' fathers. But contrary to her usual "evasion tactics," the woman finally turned herself in when the police's search pressure increased - her defense attorney emphasized this during the trial - and now finds herself inevitably confronted with the charges.

In November 2011, the woman, now 36, was sentenced by the regional court to six and a half years in prison for two counts of manslaughter. The lawyer had pleaded for five and a half years and the prosecution for seven and a half years. Thus, the court remained exactly between the two demands.

In the case of the first dead baby, the court cannot determine with certainty whether the death occurred in an exceptional psychological situation or not. Due to the extremely difficult and long birth, as well as the following trance state which the woman reported, it is to be assumed that there was reduced culpability. The court considered the death of the second baby to be manslaughter by omission, as the woman could not be proven to have actively killed the baby. Nevertheless, according to the judge, she should have taken care of a safe birth, for example, by having a second person at her side.

Both the defendant and the public prosecutor waived further appeals after the verdict was pronounced. Thus, the verdict is final.

The "Baby" homicide unit has thus reached the end of its jurisdiction - at least as far as the officers know. After the verdict, the lead investigator remarks that although they are not aware of any other undetected pregnancies, they cannot completely rule them out.

Finally, Inspector Schmidt approaches the convicted mother and offers to give her last born girl a name. And so, a second gravestone, one with a small engraving, is placed next to the baby's resting place without a name.

And lead us not into temptation but deliver us from evil.

- The Bible -

CHAPTER 9

"KILL. HER. NOW!"

The full moon illuminates the black sky and bathes the clouds that drift through the cold January night in a shadowy white. Blistering cold whips the man's face as he trudges through the streets of Berlin-Schöneberg. On his back he carries a backpack. He is looking for a suitable place, the right place. Suddenly, the man stops, lifts his head, and catches sight of a church, its spires towering high into the night sky. In front of it, a damp meadow sparkles in the moonlight. After five and a half kilometers of walking, he finally seems to have reached his destination. The frozen blades of grass crunch with every step he takes across the lawn toward the house of God. The moon is the only witness as the stranger removes his backpack from his shoulders and dumps its contents on the lawn before disappearing back into the night.

A little later, a young boy crosses Grazer Platz in Schöneberg. To shorten his walk, he decides to run across the lawn in the direction of the church. He just wants to get out of the cold winter night and into his warm home. That's all that goes through his mind as he rushes quickly across the frozen lawn.

But what is that? In the middle of the lawn, seemingly carelessly thrown down, lies a towel. And is there something else lying there? The full moon does not provide enough light for the young man to recognize what it is. His hands are fumbling in his pants pocket for a lighter. His right hand is so cold it almost hurts him as he turns the spark wheel with his thumb to get the gas to ignite. With the flame in his hand, the lad bends his knees to get a closer look at the object in front of him. A short, shrill scream escapes him as he looks into lifeless eyes. Before him, on the glittering meadow in the silver moonlight, lies the severed head of a young woman.

On this Tuesday, January 25, 1994, the picturesque moonlight is soon replaced by the blue light of the emergency services. White-red fluttering tape with the ever-repeating inscription "Polizeiabsperrung" (police cordon) stretches around the meadow in front of the church. The spotlights set up illuminate their surroundings as bright as day. Shortly after 10 p.m., the forensic pathologist on duty arrives at the site where the severed head was found. She looks at the woman's skull and carefully palpates it. Half-length strands of brown hair fall over the right half of the head's face. In her report on the find, written later, she notes: "It is a fresh head. A small amount of residual heat can be felt around the eye area."

Detectives at the Berlin-Charlottenburg State Criminal Investigation Office are faced with a mystery. Who is the woman who was killed and decapitated? Chief Inspector Christian S. must first clarify the identity of the victim - the key to any murder investigation. The experienced criminalist knows that most murderers and manslayers come from the immediate environment of their victims. And he must find the remaining body.

While Inspector S. plans his next steps, the forensic experts secure existing traces: lying next to the towel, they find other pieces of cloth, a scarf, and a T-shirt. Blood adhesions are visible on all evidence. Criminologists, assisted by patrol officers, meticulously search the area around the discovery site. They look in backyards and rummage through garbage cans. But no other objects relevant to the crime were found. Questioning residents and passers-by, as well as the young man who had found the head, led to no further clues.

On January 26, 1994, 15 hours after the discovery of the woman's head, the director of a daycare center sets out for her workplace in the Berlin district of Zehlendorf. When she arrives, she notices that one of her most reliable teachers has not come to the kindergarten that Wednesday without signing out to her or to one of her colleagues.

Immediately, an uneasy feeling creeps over the woman. She tries to reach Michaela M. on her home phone, but no one picks up the receiver. She hurriedly dialed the number of her colleague's sister. She learns from her that Michaela did not answer her phone the night before either.

It is lunchtime when the manager makes her way to her employee's apartment. She rings Michaela M.'s doorbell - over and over again, briefly at first, then she doesn't even take her thumb off the bell button. But nothing happens in the apartment. She rings a neighbor's doorbell. "Last night she didn't respond to my knocking either," the woman reports. She has a spare key, the neighbor tells her, and asks if they should look together, maybe Michaela needs help. It's not like her to be unavailable to anyone.

Heart pounding, the neighbor unlocks Michaela's door and enters the young woman's apartment. The head of the daycare center follows closely behind. They notice the telephone cord pulled out of its socket and lying across the hallway floor. Cautiously, the two women continue down the hallway until their eyes fall on one of the rooms and the lifeless body of Michaela M. The criminal investigators who are called in later note in their crime scene report, "It is clearly visible that the head of the corpse is missing." The forensic expert determines that the woman had been strangled or strangled to death. After her death, the perpetrator had cut off his victim's head.

Now investigators have the body that belongs to the severed woman's head. And a name. The task now is to find out with whom Michaela M. was in contact and, above all, had conflicts. Chief Inspector Christian S. immediately notices that there are no signs of forced entry on the victim's apartment door. "She must have known her killer and let him into the apartment herself," he mumbles to himself.

The investigator talks to Michaela's shocked and grieving sister. She tells him about her closest family member: "Michaela was a fun-loving woman. She loved going to the theater and was passionate about listening to classical music. She herself, by the way, was also very musical; she played the piano. My sister always made sure that the people around her were doing well. The neighbors liked her, especially because every now and then she would ask if anyone was bothered by her playing the piano. She was such a considerate person. But Michaela never forgot herself. Every Tuesday and Friday she went to the nearby gym. I always admired her for her perseverance and bite. For about eight years, Michaela worked at the daycare center. I know she was always honest and correct with her colleagues; yet she seemed closed off to some. But she wasn't. When she was with her family or her friends and acquaintances, she really blossomed. Michaela was a person who could quickly get in touch with others, even strangers. Nevertheless, she always remained cautious. She lived alone, after all, and every time the doorbell rang, she first looked out of the bathroom window to see who was coming to see her. She also always locked her apartment door from the inside."

Chief Inspector Christian S. listens attentively to the woman and takes notes. The sister's testimony confirms to the investigator what he already suspects: the victim knew her killer.

Michaela's sister continues: "My sister had been involved with a man, but the relationship unfortunately broke up. However, I know that she had an affair with her piano teacher Bernhard R. from September to December 1993. She took lessons with him to improve her piano playing. He then fell in love with Michaela; in any case, he wanted more from her. But my sister soon felt uncomfortable with the liaison and wanted to separate from him. He did not accept this and pestered her. Sometimes Bernhard R. would just show up at her door unannounced." A close friend of the killed and her parents also confirm to the chief inspector that there had been an affair with the piano teacher.

Spurned love is a strong motive. Did Michaela M. have to die because she did not return the affection of her piano teacher? The detective knows that he absolutely must talk to this man. For the time being, it is his hottest lead.

On Thursday, January 27, 1994, Chief Inspector Christian S. and a colleague set out for Bernhard R.'s apartment in Berlin's Schöneberg district. They arrive at around 10 a.m. and are surprised at how warmly they are greeted by the 33-year-old family man. The man makes a relaxed impression on the police officers. He seems open and approachable; speaks calmly and quietly. "Mr. R., we are investigating a homicide to the detriment of your student Michaela M. We would like to ask you a few questions and would like you to accompany us to the LKA," Chief Inspector Christian S. speaks up. "Of course, that's no problem at all," replies the piano teacher, grabs his coat, and follows the two detectives.

Arriving at the State Criminal Police Office in Keithstraße, the interrogation of the man begins at 10:45 am. The last piano lesson with Michaela M. had taken place at her home on December 6, 1993. It was St. Nicholas Day, and Michaela gave her piano teacher a calendar and a pen. There was a card with the words "Dein Wichtel" (Your Secret Santa) on it. Of course, he was happy about this attention, but at the same time it was almost too personal for him: "It's just too close for me, I can't give lessons under these circumstances. I take the view that there must always be a certain distance between me and the student." When asked if there had been other signs that the piano student was seeking his closeness, Bernhard R. answered, "Yes, I (...) already noticed that Michaela was ready to flirt. I could tell by her smile that she liked to flirt. But for me that was not a problem, to keep this at a distance. What matters is the piano lessons." That day, he said, he suggested to his student that she find another piano teacher. The reason for this was that he could not see any improvement in her piano playing.

The father of two children made a calm impression on the experienced chief inspector; there was no sign of nervousness. The detective asks the witness to reconstruct his daily routine on Tuesday, the day of the crime. Bernhard R. begins to recount: "In the morning, I was at home the whole time. My wife and my two sons were also there. Between 2:40 p.m. and 5:45 p.m. I gave some piano lessons. Then I took a break until about 18:45. During that time, I went to Hertie and bought a pack of cigarettes." Investigators take notes as the man continues, "At 18:45, my student Anna B.*, resident of Müllerstraße, appeared. The lesson lasted until 19:30. We then arranged to go to her home, as I wanted to talk to her about a contract. I took a cab home from her apartment at about 10:00 pm. As far as I remember, I paid 20 DM including tip."

Chief Inspector R. is surprised at the choice of words and the eloquence of his counterpart. The man makes an intelligent impression on him. And although the piano teacher vehemently denies an intimate relationship with Michaela, even though different people in her environment confirm it, the man is ruled out as a murderer for the investigator for the time being. As soon as they have talked to Anna B. and she confirms his alibi at the critical time, the investigators would have to start from scratch again. After Bernhard R. is released from the interrogation, Chief Inspector Christian R. sets out to track down the alibi witness. Without success. She does not answer her phone and he does not find her in her apartment. The detective decides to wait until Anna B. contacts him. He strongly assumes that she will confirm the information given by her piano teacher - who would give an alibi including a witness if it could turn out to be false within a very short time?

And indeed, Anna B. calls the LKA on the morning of the following Friday. Inspector Christian R. asks her to come in for questioning, which begins at 10:20. He tells her that she is liable to prosecution for making a false statement. But the witness confirms Bernhard R.'s alibi convincingly and in great detail. The conversation lasted only about 15 minutes. After Anna B. leaves the police headquarters, the investigating officers realize what they had already suspected: piano teacher Bernhard R. is ruled out as Michaela M.'s murderer.

Only an hour after the alibi witness was questioned, an emergency call was received at the Berlin police headquarters. On the other end of the line is a landlord who runs a pizzeria in Schöneberg. He reports that a man is standing in his store, claiming that there is a dead body in one of the rented apartments above the store. A patrol car is immediately dispatched to the address given. The officers meet a man there who makes a confused impression on them. Without further ado, he confesses that he killed Dieter K. in his apartment. He was also responsible for the murder of Michaela M. The bodies of his two victims had been possessed by Satan and only he could have saved their pure souls. He had to kill them - it was not pure murderousness that drove him, it was a work of redemption!

While the homicide squad and the forensics team investigate the crime scene in Dieter K.'s apartment and take his body to the forensics department, the alleged perpetrator is brought to the police station for questioning. But the man doesn't want to talk to anyone except Chief Inspector Christian S. When the desired investigator enters the interrogation room of the suspected murderer of Michaela M. and Dieter K., he is astonished. Restless as a tiger in a cage, the suspect paces up and down; talks confusedly. Inspector S. knows this man, who now looks like a changed man to him. Only yesterday, he had thought Bernhard R. was just an ordinary piano teacher.

Bernhard R. was born in Cologne in October 1960. His father was a trained bricklayer, but his passion was art.

His mother ran a small kiosk and provided for the family's livelihood. She turns out to be the one who forbids many things of her children. The boy grows up with his younger sister. At the age of just two, he practices playing on the piano at home. Three years later, his father teaches him to read music. In elementary school, Bernhard quickly becomes a model student. Only the subject of mathematics causes him some difficulties. If he usually gets only A's and B's, then he only gets C's in this subject. Later, he will be certified as having an above-average IQ of 120. The teachers like the boy and he quickly makes friends among his classmates. His parents enroll him in the local soccer club, but his favorite hobby remains playing the piano. At the age of 12, he takes his first professional lessons. Bernhard has big plans: he wants to become a pop star - he believes he is destined for it. On Sundays, the family goes to Catholic mass together. The boy likes these days because only then is he allowed to wear his best clothes.

Probably the most formative key experience in the teenager's life is the death of his father. Bernhard is 14 years old when his beloved father, his ally, loses his life under mysterious circumstances. After an explosion of his car, he burns to death in the flames of the wreckage. It can never be clarified whether it was an accident or a suicide. Bernhard is consumed by grief for his beloved dad. He soon gets the feeling that his mother and sister are conspiring against him. He isolates himself from family life and doesn't even share meals with the two women anymore.

When the teenager is 16 years old, he gives piano lessons himself for the first time. Bach, Beethoven, Chopin: they make his pain over the loss of his father more bearable. His relationship with his mother deteriorates, and soon they are completely estranged. At the age of 17, Bernhard has already fledged and moves to West Berlin. He has fallen in love with a girl two years his junior, with whose parents he finds shelter and who support him financially. He receives state support in the form of the Federal Education Assistance Act (BAföG) and gives piano lessons. In this way, the boy makes ends meet. A year after moving from Cologne to West Berlin, he passes his A-levels in 1979 at a grammar school specializing in music with a grade of 3.1 (C). In the meantime, he no longer has any contact with his friends in Cologne; the friendships could not survive the distance.

After graduating from high school, Bernhard moves into his first apartment, 60 square meters in the basement, and begins studying at the Hochschule der Künste (University of the Arts). He wants to become a state-certified piano teacher. For the time being, he has rejected the dream of becoming a pop star. To supplement his living during his studies, he plays keyboard in various bands at street festivals and continues to give piano lessons.

In 1982, the young man went to a gambling house for the first time. The machines with their colorful, flashing lights; the thrill of winning and losing soon take him over completely. In the meantime, his taste in music has changed. Classical music no longer touches him; jazz and pop are what he likes now. He soon loses interest in his studies. Forced de-registration follows after seven semesters in 1983.

The man in his mid-twenties is now without prospects. What should happen to him now? He finds no answer. In order to escape from reality, he drugs himself with all kinds of drugs: speed, heroin, LSD, cocaine. His music and changing female acquaintances comfort him. Even if he doesn't realize it yet: the synthetic drugs are messing up his brain chemistry.

Despite his erratic lifestyle, he meets a woman whom he marries in 1985. The couple moves into their apartment together. The couple's roles are clear: he takes care of his musical career, while she earns the money to support them together. Instead of continuing to give piano lessons, the newly married husband now concentrates again on his big dream of becoming a pop star. He composes his own songs and submits one of his lyrics to the Gema. For a short time, Bernhard manages to live without drugs. Then comes a relapse. The music career comes to nothing and, on top of that, his wife demands that he go to work and earn money as well. The misunderstood pop star-to-be does not feel that he is taken seriously.

Thus, November 6, 1986 becomes a day that Bernhard R. will remember for the rest of his life. By this time, it is clear that his wife wants to separate from him. R. was playing his piano when he felt a leaden heaviness, similar to paralysis, in his arms and fingers. Bernhard next feels a shortness of breath and has the feeling that he can no longer fill his lungs with oxygen. He describes, "Just before I would have suffocated as if by myself, I called out to God in my distress. I was just able to do it. Then I had to kneel down and put my forehead on the ground and both hands by the side of my head. Then I hear a voice. This voice was full of love and grace and this voice asked me, "Will you be my servant?" (...) This experience changed my life completely. I knew that I must never refuse such a gift."

At the end of 1987, the couple separates for good. But Bernhard is not interested in the divorce. Instead, he is driven by the question of what he must do to serve the Almighty? Bernhard R. sets out on a search. He reads the Bible and studies the Old and New Testaments in detail. In addition, he consumes amphetamines; they sharpen his mind and suppress the needs of his body. Sometimes he is awake for five days and five nights. The drug use digs big holes in his already not bulging wallet. He sells his musical instruments: keyboard, , and amplifier. The piano is allowed to stay.

Only a short time after the separation from his first wife, R. met his second wife in 1988. The wedding followed in the spring of 1989, and the newlyweds moved into a 132-square-meter apartment in Berlin-Schöneberg. On the first floor is the "Café Schöneberg," which is run by a pizza baker. Although R. returns to giving piano lessons, the money is not enough for the couple's living expenses. The social welfare office supports them.

Bernhard loves to teach other people how to play the piano, but it also exhausts him. In the summer of 1989, the couple's first son is born. Now everything becomes too much for the new father. He leaves the mother of his child and flees into the arms of another woman. He leaves his old life behind. From now on he wants to be abstinent. No drugs, no alcohol, no cigarettes. But it only takes a few months before he returns to his wife and son - that's what a father should do. His wife forgives him for breaking away from the marriage and he is allowed to move back into their shared apartment.

Bernhard is restless in his spiritual search. At first, he turns his back on the Catholic Church and joins the Protestant one. But even here he does not find what he is looking for. Instead, he joins an evangelical free church and begins preaching himself. Meanwhile, at home, Bernhard's son demands all his attention. Contact with friends and acquaintances becomes less and less due to lack of time, and because of the strain, there are frequent arguments in the marriage. Nevertheless, Mrs. R. soon becomes pregnant again. But a miracle is not only growing in her belly - her husband also experiences increasingly miraculous things in his everyday life. One day he prays so hard that his fan goes out. Another day, his prayer develops such power that a computer suddenly stops working. Even the dogs around him notice that he seems to have a spiritual power; as soon as they just smell him, they start barking. His wife is not unaware that her husband is changing, and his behavior frightens her. Every now and then she catches him waving a lighted lighter in front of her young son's face while muttering incantations to drive out evil spirits. When he tries to physically assault his very pregnant wife one day, she makes sure he is forcibly committed. Maybe, she thinks, he can be helped there.

It is February 5, 1991, when the police take Bernhard R. to a psychiatric clinic on the western outskirts of Berlin. R. reports to the experts there that he is Christ. He hears voices of demons. To drive away the evil spirits, he looks into a fire, as electric light comes from Satan. He also reports that he is being followed and bugged and that his water is being poisoned. The doctors diagnose him with paranoid-hallucinatory schizophrenia. After only two weeks, Bernhard R. leaves the psychiatric ward at his own request and responsibility. His wife and child were waiting for him at home. R. sees a psychiatrist in private practice a few more times, but then it becomes too much of a nuisance for him.

In March 1991, the couple's second son is born. The father of two starts giving piano lessons again. He gets through his daily routine without causing a stir but was seething. The never-ending search for his God-given task wears him down. He satisfies his hunger for faith from a variety of sources. Sometimes he converts to Islam. He then wants to emigrate to the USA, to the indigenous Hopi tribe, but the plan fails for lack of money. Alternatively, he turns to the mystical-religious approaches of a Swedish theosophist, who claims to have gained his knowledge from the Bible. He also has conversations with angels and spirits, before plunging into the writings of an Austrian mystic, with speculative-natural philosophical ideas. In the end, he rejoins a free church, although he does not feel that he really belongs to it.

In September 1993 Bernhard meets Michaela M. after the young woman read his newspaper ad. She takes a piano lesson with Bernhard every Monday at 6:30 p.m. for 30 marks. Student and teacher like each other right away. Bernhard R. feels he can talk to Michaela about anything, including his marital problems. Michaela thinks her piano teacher seems nice, later a little stressed, but never delusional. The music lessons take place at Michaela M.'s apartment on her own piano. In October 1993, Michaela's boyfriend breaks up with her. Her piano teacher knew this. A few days later, his student gives Bernhard a kiss on the cheek, purely amicably, but in R. the fleeting kiss sparks fierce feelings for the attractive woman. He gives her gifts and soon she even visits him in the apartment of his small family. The two sleep together. The piano teacher's wife knows about the affair but accepts it without a word or complaint. Michaela believes Bernhard will break away from his marriage and come to her, but soon learns that his wife is pregnant by Bernhard again.

For Michaela, this is a hard blow. She can't bear the idea and ends the affair with her piano teacher, asking the family man to take care of his wife and children. For her, it was all too exhausting, too complicated. But Bernhard R. cannot and will not accept the end of the relationship with his piano student. Again and again, he drives to her apartment in Berlin-Zehlendorf, even rings her out of bed at night. He wants to talk to her, but it doesn't help. On December 6, 1993, Michaela takes her last piano lesson before switching to a female teacher. She gives Bernhard a little Secret Santa gift as a farewell.

Not only is the affair with the student over, but R.'s second marriage is also about to end. His wife's third pregnancy unsettles Bernhard R. and overwhelms him even more. There is also the nagging feeling that his wife does not understand him, does not listen to him, and does not talk to him. R. seeks help at the Schöneberg crisis and counseling service. At the first meeting, shortly before Christmas 1993, the psychologist did not notice any acute crisis, unlike at the beginning of January 1994, when he visited the counseling center a second time. This second time the man makes a confused, but not delusional impression on her. He seems genuinely concerned about saving his marriage. The psychologist also notices a certain aggressiveness in her client, but he seems to have split off this belligerent side.

The more January draws to a close, the more irritable Bernhard R. becomes. He can no longer sleep. He demands that his wife leave him alone. Sometimes he wanders through the streets, addressing complete strangers with the words, "I know exactly what you're up to!"

It is Monday, January 24, 1994, when one of R.'s sons has a severe coughing fit and has trouble catching his breath. The mother remains calm; she knows her child is having a pseudocroup attack and that fresh, cool air will open the bronchial tubes again. The father, however, reacts hysterically and alerts an ambulance. The same day, he goes to the psychologist again to tell her his decision: He has decided against therapy. He then wanders aimlessly through the streets of Schöneberg.

On the following Tuesday, Bernhard R. seems to have regained his composure and the stress of the previous day appears to have subsided. Early in the evening he leaves his apartment, gets into a cab, and is chauffeured to Michaela M.'s address. At the front door, he meets the young woman who has just returned from the gym. He asks her if he can talk to her again. She agrees. Together they go into her apartment. Bernhard sits on the sofa while Michaela sits on the piano chair. "And then, very slowly and clearly, I asked a question: Can you please tell me the exact reason why you ended the relationship?" Michaela answers him. According to his memory, she talks and talks and talks, for probably three quarters of an hour. She feels too weak to fight. She doesn't feel like it and this is all too stressful. Bernhard then thinks he hears her talking badly about him, his wife, and his sons.

"That's not Michaela speaking, I thought, that's Satan himself speaking. Pure lie, lie, lie. I was absorbed in prayer, all the time." He hears Michaela speak, but he does not understand what she is saying. The woman gets up and goes into the hallway. Bernhard follows her and then has an epiphany. It hits him hard like a punch in the pit of the stomach. Michaela spurns love, she speaks ill of his loved ones, and she sucks the life force out of everyone. He knows how to protect himself through his prayers, but what about his wife, his sons? They cannot defend themselves against this possessed woman. And wasn't it only yesterday that one of his boys was in mortal danger?

"I already brought my hand near her neck, it was a pretense of tenderness, one hundred percent. (...) She suspected nothing, she suspected nothing at all. Then she suddenly said: But maybe it will still work out with the two of us. Very tenderly and lovingly, as at the time when we also loved each other physically. Then I said: What did I just hear? What did you say, why did you say that, and what does that mean?" Michaela tries to explain herself again, but he doesn't understand her in his delusion. "Then I suddenly grabbed her neck with my right hand and squeezed hard, from the front, as hard as I could, in prayer. This is very important, because I myself would not have had the strength at all, I little tiny worm of a human being, to bring this about. But if I pray in love to the one God, I will be given everything I need to do my duty. If I had not done this, little Michaela's soul could never have been saved."

While strangling the young woman with his bare hands and gazing into her eyes dilated with terror, he prays to Almighty God; asking for salvation for Michaela's pure soul, trapped in a body possessed by Satan. After his victim takes her last breath, he thoroughly washes her feet. Using the Leatherman knife he brought with him, he cuts off the killed woman's head, packs it in a backpack, and makes his way to Grazer Platz, always careful not to get too close to any dogs. He throws the knife and the backpack into a dumpster, also some of his bloodstained clothes. He burns the rest of the clothes he was wearing during the crime in the oven at home. After putting on new clothes, he leaves his apartment and gets into a cab. On the way to his piano student Anna B., he makes the cab driver stop at the address of a former lover. He also wants to "save" her soul. The only reason he does not murder this woman is the fact that she had moved to another apartment in the meantime and R. does not know her new address. Unfulfilled, he gets back into the cab.

Around 9 p.m. Bernhard R. arrives at his student's home. He confesses the murder of Michaela M. to her and asks her for an alibi. It can only be assumed why the young woman complies with her piano teacher's request. Perhaps it is the shock of the man's confession or a misperceived sense of responsibility towards his family.

The following night, Bernhard R. cannot sleep. The next Wednesday morning he has an appointment with the pediatrician with one of his sons. Around 3 p.m., he gives piano lessons to a 9-year-old girl. Late in the afternoon, he puffs a cigarette by the window and looks up at the sky. "The two big clouds looked like two animals. The top animal looked like a pig. The lower animal looked like a dachshund, which is a dog. Transferred to humans, this means: a pig is the one who plays with feelings. (...) Michaela, I only know now, was unfortunately a pig in her mental state ..."

The next day, it is 8 o’clock in the morning, Bernhard R. knocks on the door of his neighbor Dieter K. The 40-year-old unemployed man already has two promilles of alcohol in his blood when he unsuspectingly lets Bernhard into his apartment and walks into his living room with him. R. looks at Dieter K. with contempt in his eyes. He feels that this man’s life is miserable. “The decisive thing is that he could not (...) really believe in an existing God, who, however, also has everything and everyone under his absolute control.”

Bernhard says to his counterpart, “Allah will help you in your need!” Dieter looks at his neighbor suspiciously. “I don’t think so. He didn’t help with the renovations, after all!” he replies sullenly as he reaches for his pack of cigarettes and a lighter lying next to an overflowing ashtray. “I beg you not to light that cigarette!” interjects Bernhard R., because he believes that an unbeliever cannot handle poisons and would thus do himself even greater harm. Dieter K. incredulously looks at his neighbor, with the cigarette hanging in the corner of his mouth. Then he takes his lighter and turns the spark wheel until the tobacco begins to ignite and blue smoke rises. “I can do whatever I want here,” Dieter K. is enraged, before the piano teacher suddenly knocks the cigarette out of his hand and it flies across the room. K. jumps up from his sofa: “Are you crazy or what? Where’s the cigarette? Do you want it to burn everything down or what?” Bernhard points to a corner of the room. Dieter gets down on his knees and looks for the cigarette stick. “Don’t do that! Please leave the cigarette where it is!” rages the piano teacher. But the unemployed man doesn’t even think about it.

“Since he refused my last serious request - it was not a demand and not an order, it was a request, an urgent request to finally desist from this satanic aberration - I went into the position that one assumes as a soccer player when one accepts a ball directly from the air in order to send it far away from a dangerous situation into the opponent’s half. I was wearing ankle-high winter shoes and kicked him full force right in the face.”

Again and again, Bernhard R. kicks the head of Dieter K., who is lying on the ground, until his victim does not move anymore. But the murderer still has the feeling that Dieter might not be dead yet and the later autopsy confirms his assumption. Bernhard R., therefore, tries to ignite the man’s body with his lighter, but it was in vain. R. looks around his victim’s apartment and discovers an axe. Without further ado, he grabs it and goes back to Dieter K. He strikes the man’s neck several times, but somehow Bernhard R. still can’t shake the feeling that his neighbor might still be alive. Desperately, he walks through the apartment until his eyes fall on a toolbox containing a screwdriver with a yellow handle. With the tool in his hand, he goes back to Dieter K., kneels down next to him, and rams the screwdriver into his skull up to the base exactly between both eyes, because Bernhard R. suspects the "third eye", the window of the soul. To make sure that his neighbor really dies, he stuffs the lighter deep into his throat, hoping that the man will suffocate.

"Dieter K. was unfortunately a dog in his mental state. (...) In a book (...) it is written: 'He will kill the dog and the pig'. It is (...) a prophecy from the so-called Islam." After Bernhard R. has accomplished his supposed work of redemption, he once again burns his worn clothes in the oven at home. Only two hours after the brutal murder of Dieter K., the doorbell rings and Chief Inspector Christian S. and his colleague are standing in front of Bernhard R. and ask him to come to the LKA for his first interrogation.

Now, during the second interrogation, there is nothing left of the self-assurance and sovereignty of the intelligent piano teacher. During the first conversation that Inspector S. had with the man, he seemed rational. Now his behavior has turned into the complete opposite. He talks confusedly but confesses the murders of Michaela M. and Dieter K. in all details as if a movie was playing in front of his inner eye. The investigator repeatedly tells the suspect that he can call a lawyer. But Bernhard does not want to do this. For several hours, the two men talk to each other, and R. allows the criminalist a glimpse into his diseased soul. In the course of the interrogation, Bernhard R. gestures to the investigator to move closer to him. Hesitantly, Chief Inspector S. leans forward to the murderer, feeling the man's breath on his neck as he mantra-like, looking at the transcriber, murmurs to him: "KILL. HER. NOW!" An incident that still sends a shiver down the experienced officer's spine.

Anna B. is sentenced to a fine for perjured testimony, but the moral guilt weighs heavily on her shoulders since she was the first person to know about the beginning of Bernhard R.'s death campaign.

In October 1994, Bernhard R. was tried at the Berlin Regional Court. Experts certify that he is incapable of committing the crime, so that he is placed in a psychiatric clinic and the murderer is then placed in preventive detention.

Four years later, on Boxing Day 1998, the convicted murderer redeems his own soul: Bernhard R. hangs himself in the Karl Bonhoeffer Mental Hospital.

**names have been changed*

»*The source of every crime is some defect of the understanding; or some error in reasoning; or some sudden force of the passions.*«

- Thomas Hobbes (1588 – 1679), English mathematician, state theorist and philosopher -

CHAPTER 10

A phone call home

The night is illuminated by fir trees and bushes entwined with fairy lights in the front yards of local residents. On December 22, 1987, a festive pre-Christmas mood prevails in the Swabian town of Ehingen. Through many a window, one can catch a glimpse of pompously decorated Christmas trees and busy housewives diligently baking cookies. The three armed men, however, have no sense of the Christian customs that the people of Ehingen's new housing development follow. Under the cover of darkness, they secretly sneak up to the estate of the drugstore boss Anton Schlecker. Apart from the Christmas lights, no light penetrates through the windows to the outside. It seems as if no one is home. The three criminals exchange a quick glance: Perfect!

Anton Schlecker is at a small Christmas party that evening with his wife and two children. Together with family friends, the Schleckers enjoy the magic of pre-Christmas contemplation and peace. This gives the burglars enough time to enter the family home unseen and look around the premises. Their attention, however, is not focused on valuables and other precious items. They explore each room and figure out where and how they can best overpower each family member. Under no circumstances should the neighbors be startled by noise or shouting. The criminals have been working on their plan for more than half a year, and now nothing can go wrong.

Around 11 p.m., the Schlecker family returns from the party to their festively decorated home in a good mood. Father Anton parks the Jaguar in the garage and then follows his wife Christa and their children Lars and Meike into the house. The mother goes straight to the bathroom to get ready for bed. When she opens the door, she sees a man dressed in black standing in front of her. Shocked and surprised, the attractive woman with blond hair and high cheekbones cannot move at first. She is paralyzed with fear. But in a split second, adrenaline shoots through the woman's petite body and she lunges at the intruder. The latter, however, knows how to defend himself; with a firm blow to the head, he knocks the mother to the ground. The other two intruders overpower the father and the two teenagers. It is the starting signal for one of the most sensational German crimes of the 1980s.

The perpetrators don't beat around the bush; they quickly let the head of the family know what they want:

18 million marks (about 9.3 million USD) is what they want from the drugstore boss. A considerable sum. Anton Schlecker, quite the businessman, begins to negotiate with the blackmailers about the amount. At one point, they threaten to kill his wife Christa or 14-year-old Meike if he doesn't finally give them the 18 million marks. Schlecker uses one last argument: no bank has that much money in stock, which would be suspicious if he were to order such a large sum for collection now. And he hits the right nerve with the gangsters. The last thing they want is to attract attention and get caught, so the hostage and the kidnapper agree on a total of 9.6 million marks (about 5 million USD). The money is to be collected from different banks so as not to arouse suspicion. "You are a businessman, we are businessmen, you have the money, we have the goods," one of the armed criminals tells Anton Schlecker. Schlecker later states on record that the perpetrators had behaved "flexibly and cooperatively."

That night, dawn seems to be an agonizingly long time coming. The uncertainty of what would happen to them next does not allow the Schlecker family to sleep a wink in the face of their tormentors. When the new day finally dawns, two of the men force 16-year-old Lars and his sister into the garage. They take the children hostage to increase the pressure on their parents and to give expression to their demand. Lars is ordered to get into the trunk of his father's Jaguar. His younger sister Meike is told to lie down tied up in the back seat of the car. Then the two gangsters leave the estate with their hostages. Meanwhile, their accomplice guards the Schlecker couple in their bedroom.

It is only a short drive, but for the frightened Schlecker children it feels like an eternity. When the Jaguar comes to a stop, they find themselves at a wooden cabin that stands on the shore of a fishing pond in a small, wooded area. The criminals did not choose the location without reason: Although the dwelling is only 200 meters away from the main road, they can't make it out from there. Lars and Meike are terrified by the cool professionalism of their kidnappers. The two men seem to know their way around this place very well. No gesture, no spoken word used is out of place. The gangsters handcuff the siblings to the posts of a metal bed. One of the perpetrators stays behind in the small fishing hut to guard the teenagers. His accomplice gets into the stolen Jaguar and makes his way back to the Schleckers' estate.

Once there, the negotiation with the head of the family continues. Despite the threatening situation, Schlecker keeps his nerve. This later leads to whispers behind closed doors that the drugstore boss only faked the kidnapping of his children and the blackmail in order to enrich himself with the ransom sum, which is insured. It is indisputable that the amount of the loot ultimately corresponds to the maximum sum insured.

In a notebook kept by his son, Anton Schlecker details all the steps necessary for the criminals to get their hands on the 9.6 million marks, step by step. The gangsters have to work through a total of 20 items to get their loot. One of the items requires that Schlecker's authorized signatory be made privy to what is going on. He is essential for obtaining the money. Arriving at his employer's house, he is precisely instructed by him, of course in the presence of the criminals. He is to drive to three different banks in Ehingen and Ulm to collect the desired amount. With weak knees, the employee sets off. He is on the road for a while to fulfill his assignment. Enough time to start thinking wildly. Should he inform the police? Does Anton Schlecker perhaps even expect him to do so? But if the gangsters find out, would they then kill the Schlecker children? And would he then be to blame? The Schlecker employee wracks his brains as he approaches the individual bank branches. Finally, in order not to be completely idle, he implements an idea: he secretly bills down the serial numbers of the top banknotes of several bundles of money in the hope that these will later lead to the perpetrators.

The employee returns to the Schlecker store with the loot he has demanded. It is around noon when the criminals take the couple and the authorized signatory to the basement and leave them tied up. With the procurator's car, the two blackmailers and their loot drive to the small wooden house on the shore of the fishing pond to collect their accomplice. Afterwards, Lars and Meike are left tied up. When they hear the car with their kidnappers moving away from the hut, they start to free themselves. The handcuffs are not tight; they manage to squeeze their wrists through. The teenagers were in the grip of the criminals for almost 12 hours, a full 6 hours of which were spent handcuffed in the old wooden hut, until they finally find themselves back on their parents' doorstep. Meanwhile, the Schlecker couple and the authorized signatory were also able to free themselves from their handcuffs and get out of the cellar. Only now can the police be informed. The perpetrators, however, have already disappeared without a trace.

In the special department of the Tübingen criminal police, preparations for the upcoming Christmas are in full swing. None of the officers seriously believes that they still have a mission ahead of them shortly before the holidays. Until the alarm goes off. Now, none of the detectives are allowed to leave the office building; those who are already on their way home to their families are ordered back. When the team is complete, they head straight from Tübingen to Ehingen. They quickly move into their quarters and let their colleagues brief them on the current situation. A 90-member strong "Lars" special commission is set up and goes on the hunt for criminals.

The manhunt for the perpetrators is in full swing. 80 police officers search the area around the wooden hut where Lars and Meike were trapped. Seven divers search the small fishpond, looking for one of the weapons the gangsters used to threaten their victims. Perhaps the kidnappers had sunk them in the small body of water? But the search fails to uncover any objects that could put investigators on the trail of the perpetrators. Experts draw sketches of the three Schlecker kidnappers according to the family and the authorized signatory. However, it takes the pressure of a tabloid newspaper for them to publish the drawing. Detectives are not sure how similar the pictures actually look to the wanted men.

The public sends the officials 2700 tips, which must be worked through one by one. Quite a few turn out to be malicious insinuations that can quickly be shelved. Even the leads that initially seem promising and sometimes require weeks of research to check out the suspect ultimately come to nothing. And the experts are not quite able to create a profile of the perpetrator either. In addition, the criminologists are unable to find any connection between the victims and the criminals. This was probably also part of the perpetrators' plan, as the criminals thus make it more difficult for the police to identify them. Only the suspicion that Anton Schlecker might have faked the kidnapping and blackmail can be refuted by the officers. Two major points lead the criminalists to believe in the innocence of the drugstore boss: the very professional execution of the crime with its planned elements and the fact that Christa Schlecker had received a violent blow to the head.

In the 1988 winter edition of the program "Aktenzeichen XY - ungelöst, (File Number XY - Unsolved)" host Eduard Zimmermann also presents the Schlecker kidnapping to interested viewers. Because the police still have no hot lead and are left in the dark. As usual in this format, the criminal cases are re-enacted with the help of actors.

Anton Schlecker wants to help the detectives catch the perpetrators as quickly as possible. He offers a reward of one million marks. The special commission experiences a rain of clues. According to one of the officers later, the reward had led to "literally playing the lottery". But a hot lead is not there either and so the special commission "Lars" is dissolved.

Then, slowly but surely, an important connection emerges for those involved: Five years before the Schlecker kidnapping, another family went through a similar ordeal. It is March of 1982, when two heavily armed and disguised men, one of them wearing a police uniform, drive to the house of the bank director of the district savings bank in Göppingen. They kidnap the 18-year-old daughter and take her to a hut in the woods. Here, the teenager is awaited by a third man, who is also armed. He is supposed to guard the young woman. The criminals demand a ransom of 5 million marks (about 2.7 million USD) from the girl's father. Then no one would be harmed either. "Don't underestimate us, otherwise there will be a bloodbath," one of the armed criminals threatens the bank director. They leave no doubt that they will not end the hostage situation without their loot.

In the morning, the two hostage-takers set off with the head of the district savings bank in Göppingen to the bank and enter his office unnoticed. At the time, there are only 700,000 marks (about 380,905 USD) in the savings bank's safe. The gangsters are not satisfied with this. They force a money dispatcher to write a check to collect 2 million marks (about 1.1 million USD) from the state central bank. An armored car picks up the ransom money and takes it to the district savings bank, where the blackmailers receive their loot. The men flee in the bank director's company car. After the third criminal leaves the cabin in the woods and the director's daughter manages to escape, the police can be informed about the crime. By then, however, the gangsters are long gone.

And eleven years after the Schlecker kidnapping, the criminals strike again, in the immediate neighborhood of the drugstore boss. This time, their victim is the Renn family; the head of the family is a bank director. Unlike the Schlecker case, the couple is at home when two masked and heavily armed men enter their house. The couple are awakened by a noise at the balcony door, but before they can react, the burglars are in their bedroom. Mr. and Mrs. Renn look directly into the barrel of the guns, which the perpetrators point directly at their victims. They also notice the cool professionalism of the men, so they intuitively make the right decision to remain calm and act prudently. The remaining part of the night, the couple is forced to lie in their bed. One of the burglars is always with them, guarding them. When the morning dawns, the men instruct them: get up, get dressed and do their normal morning routine. The criminals don't take their eyes off the couple for a second; they even follow them to the bathroom. The intimidated hostages do not have the slightest opportunity to escape from the situation or to call for help without being noticed.

After the morning routines have played out, the criminals take their hostages to the kitchen. Mrs. Renn prepares breakfast and also offers the masked men a meal. The men refuse with a monosyllabic thank you and continue to watch the couple's activities closely. Even though everything seems so familiar and harmless, the Renn family has long since lost control of the situation. The hostage-takers leave nothing to chance. They meticulously question the couple in order to prevent any possible contact. The criminals ask when the family's cleaning lady will be on duty today. And they ask to see Mr. Renn's diary so that he can cancel all his appointments for today in good time. In all of this, the perpetrators appear to their victims to be serene, stringent, polite, almost even courteous; yet they leave no doubt about their determination.

One of the men leads Mr. Renn to the garage in the afternoon. From there, he has to cancel all pending appointments by phone. And he also calls an employee of his bank at his behest and summons him to his home. When the employee reaches the bank director's estate, he too is immediately taken hostage. In the evening, after all the stores have closed, the criminals set about further implementing their plan. Together with the Renn couple and the bank employee, the kidnappers set off in a convoy to the Volksbank's underground parking garage in Ehingen. The employee drives up in his own car; following close behind him are the kidnappers with the couple in the bank director's car. The men have exchanged their stocking masks for glued-on beards and hair wigs. Through an underground entrance, the bank's customers can easily get from the underground parking garage directly into the bank's offices. Mr. Renn has a key for this door and the bank employee in turn has the required safe key.

Mr. Renn opens the door, and the bank employee opens the safe. Inside are 2 million marks (about 1.1 million USD), which the three perpetrators stow away in bags they have brought with them. The gangsters leave the Renn couple tied up in the anteroom to the safe. The employee, on the other hand, is forced to come along as a hostage. The man is so intimidated by the criminals' cool aplomb that he does not attempt to escape when, on leaving the underground car park, the gangsters notice that they have left one of the bags behind in the bank rooms. They send the bank employee to retrieve their forgotten loot. He does as he is told without hesitation. He returns with the third bag full of money and rejoins his captors in the getaway vehicle.

The trip is short-lived. The car comes to a halt on the edge of a forest. The employee fears the worst. The criminals drive their hostage, who is scared to death, to a high seat, where they leave the man handcuffed and alone. For almost an hour, the victim sits on the high perch trying to force his hands through the handcuffs until he is finally able to free himself. Psychologically, the bank employee will be so affected by his hostage situation that he will never work in his position at the credit union again.

With this third crime, the detectives for the first time recognize a connection between the robbery of the director of the district savings bank in Göppingen and the kidnapping of his 18-year-old daughter (1982), the kidnapping of the Schlecker children (1987), and the current case, the crime against the Renn couple and their bank employee (1998). Later, it is to turn out that the gangsters were able to pursue their activities unmolested for 23 years - from their first crime in 1975, a robbery of the district savings bank Oberkochen, to the last crime in 1998 - without the police ever getting on their trail. For many people, it's hard to imagine: three men who are almost ten million richer overnight are living the perfect double life completely unsuspiciously and invisibly? Are they really supposed to have managed to commit the "perfect" crime? They are professionals in any case, at least for the criminologists there is no question about that; after all, they planned their crime so well that even the victim Anton Schlecker was suspected of being the perpetrator for a while.

Now, however, one of the criminals makes a single, but all-important mistake. Herbert Jacoby calls the bank employee's family from a phone booth, as arranged, to tell them that the father can be found in a high seat in the forest. He hangs up, picks up the phone again, and calls his home. He does not suspect that even days later it is possible to reconstruct where a phone call came from; otherwise, he would certainly not have made another call.

The investigators quickly identify the number Jacoby dialed on the second call, and that's how they get the gangster's address. From now on, the detectives shadow the suspect. After a few days, they get lucky: their target meets a man in a fancy Italian restaurant in Mannheim:

Wilhelm Hudelmaier. Two undercover investigators sit at the next table to the two crooks and eavesdrop on the conversation between the men. In fact, the two criminals talk bluntly about their latest crime. Bull's-eye! The Soko (investigation team) has been waiting for this day for almost a decade. They almost thought that they would never be able to catch the criminals. In no time, they also make out the address of the third man. Only two weeks after their last coup, the investigators invade the suspects' three apartments at the same time, early in the morning, and arrest them.

The gangsters reveal a surprise to the detectives: now that everything is over anyway, they want to come clean. They confess to 19 robberies in 23 years with a total looted sum of 20 million marks (about 10.3 million euros).

After the criminals' confession, the investigators are able to partially reconstruct their story: One of the perpetrators, Herbert Jacoby, lives in the small village of Kesten on the Moselle. Here he leads a middle-class life with his girlfriend. The man is well integrated into the village community. The Biedermann regularly stops at the "Himmeroder Hof" pub to enjoy a cold glass of beer; on Sundays, he plays skat with the neighbors. No one, not his girlfriend, relatives, friends or acquaintances, suspects anything about the millions on which Herbert Jacoby is sitting. The only thing they noticed was that the man had never held a job for two decades. The only regularity that can be observed are the walks through the neighborhood with his dog. The villagers consider Jacoby a bon vivant.

In the early 1970s, Herbert Jacoby meets his partner in crime, Wilhelm Hudelmaier. The two men are never to form a close friendship; it is more an alliance of convenience between two people whose lives are marked by failure. Hudelmaier emerges over the years as the leader of the gang. Like his younger brother Dieter, the man comes from the Swabian village of Schlichten near Stuttgart. The father of the two was once the mayor here. Although neighbors are convinced that Dieter Hudelmaier is innocent, detectives are certain that he, along with his brother Wilhelm and Herbert Jacoby, is the third member to complete the gang. Acquaintances of the younger brother, on the other hand, believe that Dieter was forced into the deeds by Wilhelm. After all, he had always been a rascal. They say that he committed his first burglary in Switzerland at the age of 18.

Hudelmaier and Jacoby committed their first crime, initially as a couple, 12 years before the Schlecker kidnapping. On March 7, 1975, the two men, who are around 40 years old, rob the district savings bank in Ebersbach near Esslingen. For disguise, they wear glued-on beards and wigs. One of them points a pistol at the employees, the other a shotgun. They get away with

195,000 marks (about 100,000 USD). But there is one thing the two robbers haven't thought of: a bag in which to stash the money. A cleaning bucket standing around helps, and they stuff their loot into it before disappearing.

Just four months later, in the summer of 1975, the two men rob the district savings bank in Oberkochen. This time they also have a backpack with them for the stolen 135,000 marks (about 75,000 USD). In November 1975, they robbed the German Bank in Esslingen for 104,000 marks (approx. 60,000 USD). Robbery after robbery followed; by 1978, the two robbers had taken 2.6 million marks (approx. 1.4 million USD). Although the criminals have accumulated a considerable arsenal of weapons over time, from submachine guns to pump guns, they never fire a single shot or physically injure any of their victims during their crimes.

After the bank robberies, Herbert Jacoby disguises himself again with his bourgeois, inconspicuous life. Wilhelm Hudelmaier, on the other hand, regularly absconds abroad. He possesses a forged Canadian passport in the name of William Meyer. After the Schlecker coup, this is his ticket to the United States. His little brother Dieter, who was an accomplice in the robbery of the bank manager of the district savings bank in Göppingen and the kidnapping of his 18-year-old daughter, as well as in the Schlecker kidnapping, does the same to Jacoby; he, too, disappears into his bourgeois life.

Wilhelm, the head of the gang, on the other hand, really enjoys himself in America. His lifestyle is extravagant - expensive cars, boats, and pretty women. With the looted millions he not only buys a villa in California; he also buys an exclusive sailing yacht. Luxury is expensive and so his part of the loot is soon used up. Although the crook tries to invest his money profitably in a legal way, these attempts fail miserably. But that's not the only thing weighing heavily on the man: since the mid-1980s, he has known that he is suffering from blood cancer. At the beginning of the 1990s, he has to be treated in a clinic to save his life. This procedure is not only physically and psychologically exhausting and lengthy, the radiation and chemotherapy that cure him also cost a lot of money. The seriously ill man does not have health insurance.

After his successful battle against cancer, Hudelmaier moves into a two-room apartment in Mannheim. From now on, the wild, luxurious years are a thing of the past. Now the money is not even enough to buy the things of daily life. And so it happens that the aged hoodlum, together with his accomplice, plans the robbery of the Renn family; unaware that it is to be their last coup.

The trial of the three criminals gets a lot of attention from the press and the public. Everyone is curious to find out what the three men, who committed one crime after another for more than 20 years without the police getting on their trail, look like. Some even talk about the crooks with a certain respect in their voices, after all, their case is exceptional because of the large number of crimes and also because of their ingenuity. Although the three men committed serious crimes, some journalists write of the "gentleman gangsters." The lawyer for the joint prosecution cannot deny this impression when he first encounters Wilhelm Hudelmaier: "This can't be a blackmailer! This is an honest, brave Swabian! He had manners, a well-groomed, quite calm man and intelligent." But the lawyer corrects his opinion after a conversation with the criminal - he is overcome by the feeling that "this is a stone-cold guy".

When the three defendants enter the courtroom for the first time, there is blank amazement in the auditorium as three old-looking men, between 60 and 64 years old, shuffle into court. They give the impression of going on a pensioner's outing. The potential danger attributed to them simply cannot be assumed from their appearance, but the judges are not fooled. Though the majority of their crimes have fallen victim to the statute of limitations, the presiding judge sentences Wilhelm Hudelmaier and Herbert Jacoby each to 13.5 years in prison. Dieter Hudelmaier is put behind bars for 7.5 years.

For the head of the gang, the sentence is tantamount to life imprisonment, for only one year after his imprisonment, Wilhelm Hudelmaier dies as a result of his cancer. Herbert Jacoby withdraws from the public eye after his release around 2013, and Dieter Hudelmaier disappears from radar. The Schleckers, on the other hand, continue toappear in the press a few times, though the family-run drugstore chain announces its insolvency in June 2012. The ransom money from the Schlecker kidnapping never resurfaced.

Concluding words of the author

» Those who keep good things to themselves leave the digital marketplace to the troublemakers. «

Dear Reader,

Thank you for holding this book in your hands. We hope you enjoyed it and that it successfully drew you to Germany's darkest side. If so, please leave a positive review on Amazon right now and feel free to introduce this book to your friends. Without positive reviews, books won't be found in the digital marketplace these days. Reviews are the spotlight of the virtual world. With your support, you are giving us more pleasure than you can imagine.

We are counting on you.

Thank you very much in advance.

Sincerely,

Adrian Langenscheid and Benjamin Rickert

Email: AdrianLangenscheid@mail.de

Instagram: @truecrimedeutschland

TRUE CRIME INTERNATIONAL:

The Successful Book Series
By Adrian Langenscheid

His distinctive style and the success of his books made Adrian Langenscheid one of the most successful true crime authors in Germany. Have you enjoyed this book? If so, feel free to order the other books and help other readers immerse themselves in the world of true crime by writing a review.

Did you like this book? If so, I would be happy to give you another of my publications as a gift. To do so, please sign up for my "true crime" newsletter. In the future, you will not only receive spam-free information from me, but you can also download the eBook "True Crime Best of Adrian Langenscheid" as a special welcome and thank you.

You can find the newsletter at:

https://www.subscribepage.com/truecrime or just scan the qr-Code.

Yours sincerely, Adrian Langenscheid.

Printed in Dunstable, United Kingdom

78941966R00139